PRIVATE EYE

CRAIG BROWN'S
IMAGINARY
FRIENDS

Parodies
2000 – 2004

PRIVATE EYE

CRAIG BROWN'S
IMAGINARY FRIENDS

Parodies
2000 - 2004

For Lizzy, Molly and Peig
and in memory of Adam Shand Kydd

Published in Great Britain by
Private Eye Productions Ltd
6 Carlisle Street, London W1D 5BN

© 2004 Pressdram Ltd
ISBN 1 901784 37 1
Designed by Bridget Tisdall
Printed and bound in Great Britain by
William Clowes Ltd, Beccles, Suffolk

2 4 6 8 10 9 7 5 3 1

Contents

Foreword by Max Clifford

Have you ever seen a tot in tears, a poorly tot of three or four years of age – in tears?

Well, I have. And it cuts me up, it really does.

That's why I've spent my entire professional life doing my darnedest to make folk happy. And not just the tiny tots – sometimes it's the mums and dads and dear old nans who can do with a bit of cheering up too!

Do you know anyone who's under the weather or down on their luck? Perhaps someone who's just done something they truly regret?

If so, give us a bell soonest. I'll have the full story on all the front pages by the morning. Believe me, it'll cheer up the Great British Public – tots, nans, the lot – no end.

You know, I'll never forget the time Elvis Presley got in touch.

"Max," he said, "I'm the undisputed King of Rock 'n' Roll. But I've eaten far more than is good for me and I've taken many too many pills and now I'm sitting on the toilet and I'm frankly not feeling my best. As my oldest friend in the business, Max, I'm hoping you'll be able get me out of this pickle."

Sadly, I was stuck on the other phone at the time. I was talking to a senior member of the Royal Family who shall remain nameless. So by the time I got to hear Elvis's message, he had already passed away.

But the story has a happy ending. Luckily, I was able to tip off the gentlemen of the press – The Sun ran Elvis's tragic death as a front page exclusive. I'm proud to say that, thanks to my quick reactions, the following week his Greatest Hits record went straight to Number One in the charts!

The writer of this present tome is in the happiness business too. Like yours truly, he's always been a lovely shoulder to cry on.

Top celebrities – writers, pole-dancers, politicians, glamour models, all-round family entertainers – confide in him.

They tell him their dreams and their fears.

And they trust him with their innermost secrets.

Now he's letting us share in those secrets of a lifetime – "as told to Craig Brown". Yes, the guy's giving something back to society. And I for one salute him for it.

And you know what? If this book brings a smile to the face of just one tot, just one little tiny tot, it'll have all been worthwhile.

Cheers!

H.M. The Queen

A knock on the door. It is my son, Edward.

"Hello Edward," I say, informally.

"Hello Mummy," he replies.

We shake hands. What's that expression everyone uses these days? That's it. We are a close-knit family.

"Have you come far?" I ask.

"Not really," he says, "We don't live all that far away. Though the traffic was quite busy."

"There are a lot of cars on the roads these days" I say. "You sometimes wonder where they are all going!"

"Yes!" he agrees.

We have a smile.

"You can't help but wonder," he says, "where they are all going!"

"Yes!" I agree.

I have been working on my Christmas message. It is not going well.

"Traditionally, Christmas is the season when many of us, young and old alike, take stock of the year that has passed and ask ourselves why we bother..."

"Christmas is a time when our thoughts inevitably turn to family. We ask ourselves, over and over again, why just one or two of them can't for the life of them sometimes do something right for a change..."

"In this, my Jubilee year, as I have travelled up and down the length and breadth of the country I have had occasion to meet a great many of you. Time and time again I have been struck by the very real way in which you just stare at me as though I were some sort of performing seal..."

I can't seem to hit the right note. Perhaps I will have a little lie-down.

It has been an odd sort of year.

In August, there was an intruder on the Palace roof, making a terrible racket with an electric guitar.

I asked who it was.

It turned out to be an old woman called May.

Needless to say, once one had got in, there was no stopping them.

By the end of the day the garden was absolutely jam-packed and no one could do anything about it. One simply had to grin and bear it.

But I didn't really bother to grin.

I saw a lot of the Prime Minister during the past year. We have regular meetings. He greatly values my tremendous wealth of wisdom and experience.

It is my duty as Monarch to advise and inform. "My son

Edward pointed out that there was an awful lot of traffic on the roads this morning," I tell him.

"That will be the cars," he says.

"And lorries," I say. Lorries are for putting things in.

"Yes. Cars and lorries," he agrees. Once again, he has been able to draw on my vast wealth of experience.

"People getting from A to B," he adds.

That doesn't sound very far, I point out.

"They might be better off walking," I say, giving it some thought. "Perhaps the third lane of the motorway could be reserved for pedestrians, with cars and lorries in the first."

The Prime Minister says that is one idea he has never thought of.

He will look into it.

I am pleased my idea seems to have 'caught on'.

"...which would leave the second lane free for horses and carriages and so forth," I add.

I ask after his wife: "How is Norma?"

They do appreciate it when one shows a bit of personal interest. He says his wife is very well.

"Well, goodbye," I say, getting out of my chair, shaking his hand and leaving the room. This is his signal to depart.

"Happy Christmas, Charles," I say, shaking his hand and presenting him with a neatly-wrapped blue tie.

"Super," he says.

"I trust it fits," I say.

"Happy Christmas, Andrew," I say, shaking his hand and presenting him with a neatly-wrapped yellow tie.

"Super," he says.

"I trust it fits," I say.

The other two get ties too. "You can always use yours to muzzle that dog of yours," I say to Anne.

"Fair enough!" she laughs.

We go into lunch.

"I'm not eating off this," says Philip. "It's bloody plastic."

I look down. He is right. Our plates are made of plastic, and so are the knives and forks.

I pull up the cloth. Beneath it is a trestle table.

At this point, Charles mentions that Edward and Andrew are both sitting on chairs brought in from the garden.

I call the butler over. "What happened to our silver and our dining table and our chairs?" I ask.

"Out of harm's way," he says, with a wink.

Like many grandmothers, I'm afraid I spoil my grandchildren at Christmas.

A shiny ten pence piece with their Christmas cards.

And Christmas "crackers" – one each – after lunch.

I stow their paper hats safe in a box, so they can be clean-on next year.

After lunch, we all feel rather merry. I turn to my daughter Anne.

"Anne" I say, "Do tell us that story of the time your dog savaged those people in the park!"

"Oh, go on, tell us, Aunt Anne!" chorus my grandchildren.

It is one of her favourite stories. She always tells it so well.

By the end, we are all in fits.

I call the butler over. "I think we might have our coffee sitting on the armchairs in the drawing room," I say.

"What armchairs?" the butler replies.

Martin Amis

I am a serious.

It is novels that I usually write: what I usually write is novels. And you know why I write? I write to fill the chiliastic lacuna of the aberrant psychotheatre in my headipops.

And it all adds up to one thing.

I am a serious.

Iosif Stalin. Beast and Monster. Mass-murderer. What do we need to call him? What is it necessary to call him? Stalin is too simple: too simperbubble. In considering our selection of an appropriate word, I must first contend that the simple word "Stalin" does nothing to convey the guy's sheer horrid horridity. Let's think again: let's reinvent the language to form a noose around his head.

Mister Walrus Whiskers. That just about does the trick. I can candidly argue that, following a great deal of research, I know he wouldn't want to be called Mr W-W: not one little bit. Or what about "Starling"? No way, Jose Feliciano. It sounds too like a bird: and a bird he was most certainly not.

The guy hated flying: hated it. Nor can we call him by his matey primonomenclaturalition, which is, of course, Iosif: Iosif is no mate of mine.

And why, pray, is it necessary to point out at this post-millennial juncture that Iosif Stalin – or Starling – is no mate of this 52-year-old male novelist? Or, to put it another way: *Novelist male old year 52 this of mate no is – Starling or – Stalin Iosif that juncture this at out point to necessary it is, pray, why and?*

It can here be stated, boldly and fearlessly: Iosif Stalin was a very bad man. And my contention goes further, and can herein be tersely stated: he wasn't nice at all.

Journey with me, if you will, back to 1974. The now-legendary offices of the New Statesman. Every major young writer and thinker in the world was by chance foregathered therein: Barnsey, Hitch, La Fent and my own good (I herewith employ the adjective in its post-Augustinian sense) self. Brazen young intellectuals, we would throw ideas around like frisbees, these frisbideas or ideabees swoop-swirling around the office and smashing coffee-cups before being caught and tossed back in the general direction – gendire – of myself, the original tosser.

Stalin – let's, for the sake of argumentables, call him Stalin – Stalin was mentioned in the intellectual ferment of those offices only once.

"Hey, Hitch," I gobspoke one day, reading a newsypaperium while Hitch was nibbing a characteristically finely-wrought yet deeply impassioned essay on the fraught situation on the Surrey/Sussex border (it was some years before he would discover South America), "Hey, Hitch – ever heard of a guy called Stalin?"

A moment's lacuna. A second's void. A sixtieth-of-a-minute's diaspora.

Then:

"Yeah! Stalin! I dig that one-hep crazy dude!"

It was not until the year AD 2000 that I discoverbubbled exactly how wrong Hitch was, and that Iosif Stalin – Walrus Whiskers – was in fact not nice at all.

Let me repeat that.

Not.

Nice.

At.

Allipegs.

Trotsky. Trotski. Half his name sounds like a horse. The other half is a mass-produced brand of fruit-flavoured yoghurt.

So henceforth and heretowith, it is, I would contend, both tempting and appropriate, in this day and age, all things considered, to call him....Comrade Horse-Yoghurt.

Was Comrade Horse-Yoghurt as evil as Walrus Whiskers? Was he? And how do both of them compare to Adolf Hitler, whom reputable historians correctly identify as the German Chancellor from 1933-1945?

Put it this way: put it this way. On an Evil Scale of one-to-ten, in the cold light of day (never colder than when night beckons) how do these three men – Horse-Yoghurt, Walrus Whiskers, and Adolf Littler (he was half an inch smaller than the other two) rate?

This is my reckoning, my total, my final score count-up, on the Scale of Evil:

H.Y. Trotsky: 7 out of 10

A.L. Hitler: 9 out of 10

W.W. Stalin: 10 out of 10.

So I would contend, gentlemen, that from this chart, it is indeed necessary to conclude that the overall winner – not just evil, but mega-evil, and not just mega-evil but megaleggahegga evil – is W.W. Stalin. By at least ten per cent.

How to register the size, the immensity, the extent of his evil? Exertions of the imagination are called for.

Imagine a blank piece of paper. White: white. Very, very, white.

Now imagine an ink-blot: a black ink-blot.

And there you have it. Iosif Stalin. Evil as an ink-blot.

Or – imagine it – still more evil: more eviller still.

I am a serious.

Wherever he is now – and one sincerely hopes and trusts that he is at present floundering in the darkest reaches of Hell, doubtful though the actuality of that post-life domicile may be – then I hope Stalin has read these words, these sentences, these paragraphs and chapters, and finally this book, of mine.

And I further hope this: this I further hope.

I hope the guy feels thoroughly ashamed of himself.

A theory: a theory of mine. Stalin, Walrus Whiskers, Koba the Dread, whatever, actively enjoyed being not just evil but deeply unpleasant. He gorged on unpleasantness, on not-niceness, like a bear feeds on wild berries or an antelope feeds on mice (check).

So, there we have it, Comrade Hitch (if I may)! You were wrong: I am right. I am right: you are wrong. But no hard feelings, emotions, thought-yelps. Next time you're over, let's slurp down a few alco-jars at the local hostelry. But, if you don't mind let's on no account (no: account) invite Comrade Stalin!

Yours ever,
Martin Serious

Heather Mills

U sing my special friends-and-family key, I let myself into Buckingham Palace and put my head round the Queen's sitting room door.

Elizabeth tells me she's been hurting dreadfully and has lost her sense of identity. "I'm, like, who am I?" she says. She always turns to me for comfort. She finds me very down to earth. "You're a very caring person, Heather," she says, "Probably too caring for your own good. When my time comes, I hope they'll make you Queen. It's what Diana would have wanted, and to replace me they'll need someone well known throughout the world for her tireless charity work."

I'm like, "I couldn't be Queen, that's not my style, I'm not up to it." But she gets me sat down and says, "You've spent your whole life caring for others, Heather. And it's time you got them to care for you. You'd fit this throne real beautiful – and what's more for all the love you've got inside you, you deserve it, love".

It wasn't always like this, you know. These days, people like the Queen are queuing up to see me, but when I was a child we were very, very poor. It was like Steptoe and Son, we were that poor. Poorer. In fact, now you mention it I remember actually being brought up by Steptoe and Son, only they never showed me on the scenes they showed on the television, because the old man Steptoe locked me in a cupboard for the six years they were filming. Sometimes you could hear a bump and a yell, but that's the only sign the viewers ever had that I was in there.

Then they put me to work up the chimneys. I was a chimney sweep till the age of 11, going up the chimneys and coming down all like black and sooty. Luckily, I ran away from my wicked employer and leapt into a river, and luckily I was transformed into a water baby, where I met others in the same situation – and from them I learnt the meaning of love.

From there, aged sort of 13, I went to live in Elm Street, where the nightmare took place. I never trusted Freddy Krueger, there was just something about that way he used to kill people at random that I didn't like.

So I thought, no, I'm not having any of this, and I managed to save a helluva lot of kids from his clutches. I never told anyone that before, but that's one of the reasons I'm being considered for the Nobel Peace Prize this year, which is great.

Paul's been a lot happier since we got wed. He now says he couldn't have written some of his greatest songs, like *Yesterday* and *Satisfaction*, if it wasn't for me. *Martha My Dear* was about me, and so was *Mull of Kintyre*. Now I hear they're planning to call me the fifth Beatle, which is great, because of all my behind-the-scenes work, which I've never spoken of before now. Like, I don't want to overshadow all the work John Lennon put into the band, 'cos I've got a lot of respect for John, so let's just say a lot of the tunes were basically mine, and leave it at that, shall we?

I'd like to clear one thing up for good and proper, right. I get along with Paul's kids great, we're very, very close, in fact Stella calls me her angel, because I design all those clothes for her. By the way, the last time I saw Mother Teresa, like, she greeted me like a sister and she said she'd love me to design her a really beautiful evening frock, which was basically a great compliment coming from her.

———————————

One of the reasons Paul respects me is because before we got married I was obviously a whole lot more famous than he was – face it, I'd been a top model and international charity worker for ten years – and I made sure that I didn't push him into the spotlight, because that's like quite hard to handle if you're not used to it. So the papers were full of 'Heather Mills's New Guy' and 'Heather to Marry' and 'Who's the Lucky Man?' and all that stuff, but I never let it go to his head, which is great.

Sure, I've had my share of hardships. It wasn't much fun coming face to face on that dark, stormy night with the Loch Ness Monster armed only with a pencil and an elastic band, I can tell you. And the day I went up to Saddam Hussein, looked him straight in the face and said, "You've got to let some love into your world" – believe me, that took some nerve. By the way, after just ten minutes he asked me to marry him, begged me, just like every other guy, but I was married to Paul, right, and that's not the kind of person I am. But I sometimes think that if I'd said yes, perhaps there wouldn't be all this sort of tension in the world, which is a shame really.

———————————

I don't usually talk about this but I was abducted by aliens aged 15 and a half and it wasn't at all pleasant really. It was when

I was 14. I was just walking down the street one day, wondering how I was going to earn enough money to pay for a great holiday at Disneyland for all the other poor kids in the world when this space ship came down and abducted me. And I was only 13 at the time. I'll never forgive my alien abductors the way they treated me – clean this, clean that, do this, do that, the lot.

But when you suffer in life, you go one of two ways. You're either like, "I've been mentally and physically abused by aliens, I'm going to get really angry and abusive and get eaten up with it." Or you're like, "No, I'm going to make a difference, I'm going to put all the love I feel inside me into helping others less fortunate than myself and if that means becoming the world most famous international charity worker in the process then that's something I'll just have to come to terms with in my own way and if some people don't like that well they'll just have to lump it."

So now when people say to me, "Even with your seemingly unlimited capacity for caring, Heather, will you ever be able to forgive those aliens who abducted you when you were only 11?" I say, "They made me who I am today, and though I'll never voluntarily return to their flying saucer, and though I disapprove of many of their methods, I hope they'll come some day to understand what I wrote in that song all those years ago, like, 'All you need is love – love is all you need'." And you know something? I've taught Paul how to play that song, and now he accompanies me whenever I sing it. He's a great guy, and you know what? I'm determined to use my fame to bring him to the world's attention.

Chapman Brothers

Jake Chapman: For the past seven years we have been trajectorising the downsize of the paradigm shift in our culture in a work-in-progress called –

Dinos Chapman: Fuckface. It's called Fuckface. It's basically like kind of a pubescent face with two penises where the eyes should be.

Jake: Essentially it represents an attempt to recuperate the issue back to the reclassication of its own symptoms vis-a-vis the recuperation of an attempt at representation.

Norman Rosenthal: Marvellous! I find it a tremendously powerful work. I am amazed by it and find it really incredibly beautiful. One has this pubescent face, and instead of eyes it has, it has, it has –

Jake: Cocks.

Rosenthal: Quite. Quite. It's a very complex work of art, full of ambiguity and eternal contradiction. On the one hand, we have this pubescent face, and on the other hand, on the other hand we have, we have –

Jake: Cocks.

Sir Nicholas Serota: Fuckface explores issues of colonialism, capitalism, racism and globalisation in the early part of the 21st century. It poses very real questions about the hypocrisies inherent in our contemporary post-9/11 culture, and, if I may say so, boys, is fuelled by your unerring instinct for cultural anxiety, extenuated and enhanced by a darkly ironic –

Dinos: Wanker.

Serota: Mm?

Dinos: Wanker.

Serota: Wanker? That's not in my current catalogue. Is it perchance a work-in-progress? It sounds very exciting, and if at all possible on its completion I greatly look forward to viewing it.

Dinos: No. You're the wanker.

Serota: Me? Oh! Marvellous! That's to me a very thrilling, very... stimulating observation, offering plenty of food for thought at this, the apex of a cultural tide-change.

Rosenthal: Boys, boys, boys. You called him a wanker. Why didn't you call me a wanker too? Go on, say it, I can take it – it's because you don't like me, isn't it?

Jake: Tosser.

Rosenthal: Me? Tosser?

Jake: Yeah, you – tosser.

Rosenthal: Oh, thank you, thank you. With that dark irony of yours, I must say you really do transcend your age, boys.

Serota: Which artists do you have an innate, as it were, taking the dialectic into account, inherently, looked at in a highly visceral way, would you say, ah. Let me put it another way, who are your favourite artists?

Jake: Not Picasso.

Dinos: He was, like, an ape with an easel, an ape with its head cut off by an axe, or piano-wire, or slowly sawed off with this great big –

Jake: Picasso knew nothing about art. He was just a deeply cynical and incredibly vulgar little Spaniard.

Rosenthal: Oh dear. One has always rather admired him. Up to now. But I'm tremendously grateful to you both for showing me the error of my ways, as it were. I suppose, on reflection, Picasso is somewhat flawed. In terms of his... well, his perception of reality. And so forth.

Dinos: Rembrandt's pretty good crap, too.

Jake: Rembrandt! Ha! He appeals exclusively to all those little old ladies with their little old hats and coats, twittering nonsense, stuffed full of Prozac and PG Tips while they await their turn to be released from their vacuous parasitic lives in some hermaneutic hospital ward peopled by so-called medical staff remorselessly dedicated to the long overdue murder of worthless citizens.

Dinos: Adolf Hitler was a good artist.

Jake: Within the severe societal constraints of the outmoded representational watercolour genre. But at least his vision was transgressive, unlike some I could name.

Serota: Adolf Hitler! That's a profoundly original thought! Deeply disturbing, yes – but also HUGELY exciting! I welcome this bravura debate. Indeed I do. It's by turns shocking, amusing, stimulating, powerfully provocative and *viscerally horrifying.*

Dinos: And Harold Shipman. He was a good artist, for a doctor.

Serota: Ah, yes – Shipman! A most necessary reminder that the inclusion of his work on The Turner Prize shortlist is really long overdue. Some might find it shocking, yes – but then it has always been the artist's duty to shock. Now, tell me, lads – what are you working on next?

Jake: We're exploring the spineless manner the liberal intelligentsia, particularly those of them working within the mileu of the visual arts, are happy to sacrifice all their beliefs, aesthetic, philosophic and moral, in order to lick the arses of the modish and the celebrated.

Rosenthal: That sounds marvellously complex and ambitious, exploring powerful new territory in a way that is both, er, powerful, er, yes, powerful and new and, er, yes, deeply exploratory.

Serota: This new work. What does it, as it were, *involve?*

Dinos: Basically, it's a conceptual work called PISSPOT involving Jake and me tanking ourselves up –

Jake: – that is, passing an extreme volume of liquid down the oesophagus into the stomach –

Dinos: – then waiting a few hours until we are both fit to burst –

Jake: – then asking you two gentlemen –

Dinos: – namely you, Wanker, and you, Tosser –

Jake: – to lie naked on the gallery floor –

Dinos: – while we pull out our male genitalia –

Jake: – and piss all over you.

Serota: So you are, in a very real way, aestheticising the act of urination, turning what society regards as an essentially private act into something very real and very public. To me, PISSPOT explores crucial issues, posing profound questions whilst refusing to provide easy answers.

Rosenthal: But you're not going to urinate over Serota first are you? That's SO unfair! It's MY turn! I'm just as good at being pissed over as he is! Okay, I'm not playing any more!

The Duchess of Devonshire's Chatsworth Cookbook

My uncle Stiffy, who lived for a lightly-poached tongue, had strong views on food. "Never remove the gunk from a trotter before boiling it," he would say, whilst tending to a particularly troublesome toe-nail with a fine 16th century silver corkscrew, "There's oodles of nutrition in filth."

At Chatsworth, we take care to remember Uncle Stiffy's maxim whenever we boil a trotter. This is what makes this receipt so particularly tasty.

TROTTER ON HORSEBACK
1 pig's trotter

2 onions

2 pints water

2 slices "Mother's Pride"

Do make sure your pig is completely dead before removing its trotter. Great Aunt Squinty forgot, and lost an eye as a consequence. Thankfully, the eye boiled up well, and made an interesting addition to the fruit salad we served on Coronation Day. Waste not, want not, as our old Governess used to say.

If ever she came across a dead insect – a bluebottle or wasp – she would never dream of throwing it away. After all, what is a Lemon Curd without insects?

First, discard the onions. You will not be needing them for this receipt.

Now boil the trotter in the water for 10-15 minutes, but not a second longer. It should remain nice and chewy, with that delicious trottery flavour.

Wrap it in the two slices of Mother's Pride, buttered to taste. Serve warm-ish. Ideal for a late breakfast, or perchance as that "little something extra" for afternoon tea.

My husband Andrew is easy to feed, thank goodness, and seldom complains about what is put before him. On Shrove Tuesday last year, he polished off one of our new table-mats under the impression it was one of chef's pancake efforts.

Unlike me, Andrew is a terrific pudding person. He also particularly loves what people on television will insist upon calling "seafood". This dish succesfully combines his two great passions!

JELLYFISH CUSTARD
1 small to medium jellyfish

2 pints water

*Custard, preferably from milk fresh
from your own herd*

Bring the water to the boil. Chef will show you how. Now plop the jellyfish into it.

Boil for ten to fifteen minutes, until it has stopped wriggling.
Dollop your lovely fresh custard all over it.

Serve with either freshly-baked crackers or a crisp garden
salad, depending on season.

———————————

My sister Diana was a great judge of mousse. Diana and her
husband Oswald, who was a huge success in politics, would always
serve a liver mousse to start a meal, and often a fruit or cheese
mousse to close it. Diana always said that the secret of the perfect
mousse was to find the very best mousse chef and leave him be.
Incidentally, she always insisted that the second 's' in mousse
remained silent, and would grow simply livid if any of her guests
lingered a moment too long on theirs.

This particular mousse receipt is named after a dear old
friend of Diana's from the pre-war years. How very long ago it all
seems now!

MOUSSE DE ADOLF
7 hard-boiled eggs

7 fl.oz double cream

¾ pint mayonnaise

2 tablespoons dry vermouth

Stir the mixture with a spoon for a minute or two, then pass it
over to chef, who will know what to do.

Diana always used to say that for all his faults, Adolf always left
his plate spotless, particularly when his favourite mousse was
being served. It is all too easy to criticise him, and in many ways
he was far from pleasant, but this is the sort of thing chefs really
appreciate.

I sometimes wonder what happened to good manners.
Nowadays, a good many visitors to Chatsworth seem content to
leave gubbins on the side of their plate. Of course, an ingenious
chef can always think of a way of re-using these gubbins in a stew

or "hot-pot", but that is not the point. There is no excuse for a messy plate.

Lady Blanche lived in Dieppe for the sake of economy. Aunt Natty, as my parents called her, had strong views on French food, and would insist on all her meals being cooked in England, then sent over by ferry.

This caused her dinner parties to be beset by delays. If one were invited to luncheon on Friday, one could not expect the principal dish to arrive at the earliest before dinner on Sunday.

LADY BLANCHE'S FISH PIE

1 Tin Sardines

Mashed potato

Ask a willing hand to open the tin of sardines for you. Now place the contents in a serving dish. I have noticed over the years that some guests enjoy crunching on the backbone of a tinned sardine, while others do not. One can always remove the backbones from the general mix. Threaded together and painted in lovely deep blues and reds, they make a most attractive table decoration.

Spoon the mashed potato over the top of the sardines and scatter with eggs from the garden. Aunt Natty would always insist on wearing flippers and a snorkel, saying it was the only way to eat fish pie, but sadly in the present day many people have lost the knack of eating in snorkels, and the fashion nowadays is to eat without.

Michael Moore

Don't get me wrong. I love Britain. Love it. And not just because it begins with a B and ends with an N – just like BUN, my numero uno favorito mid-morning snack!

And while we're on the subject of buns, many of my good friends who happen to be poor like to eat them too – and that's great news. In fact, research proves that 20% less people in the USA commit a serious felony while eating a bun.

So why, I hear you ask, doesn't Bush distribute buns free – thereby cutting crime by 80% at a stroke? Right first time: the guy's under the thumb of the corporate chocolate cookie lobby – and they sure as hell don't want to see the shares in their alternative mid-morning snack go through the floor.

Where was I? Oh yeah. Britain – and how I just love the place. And you Brits love me in return – hey, guys, my book's still right up there at Number One in your best-seller lists, so how the hell could I not love you? Spread the word.

But first let me ask you a simple question. So, um, why exactly is it you guys don't kick shit at the idea of living under a fascist dictatorship? Not once – not EVER – has anyone come up to me in the wonderful streets of London and having thanked me for impacting their lives, etc, said to me, "Gee Whizz, Mike, you've done some great things in your movies and in your best-selling books – but it's hard as hell living under the iron boot of a fascist dictatorship."

Whyever not? Hey, guys – get a life, willya? Now, I don't intend to waste time rehashing the past 1000 years of British history. Whaddya think I am – a nerd or something? But here's something you sure as hell should know about your country:

FACT: For the past years, Queen Two's husband, Tony, has secetly imprisoned nearly 1000 – that's 1000, goddammit! – political dissidents at an address in London's Marylebone Road.

Just last year, I took my cameras to this top-secret location – Codename Tussaud. Well, hey, guess what? It's a building without windows – your Rulers have sure been studying their Stalin. Having exchanged some of my own money for a ticket, I barged my way past the dumbstruck doorman. What I then saw put a chill in my soul (not my SOLE, dumbo – my sneakers may be inexpensive, but just this minute they're warm as Mom's cherry pie!!). Inside, I was confronted by rows of former statesmen, rock stars and social agitators – each one of 'em forced to stand still for hours at a time, and not even permitted to blink, dammit. And let me tell you this: those guys looked ILL.

"So hey, Mike – what's the big deal? Why should we care about a bunch of guys imprisoned by the Blair regime in a secret address in North West London? What's that to do with us?"

Oh, sure – right now, I guess you have a hundred good excuses for not caring. Right this minute, Christina Aguilera might be swinging her pretty little butt on MTV. That's not just one good excuse – it's two! But why not set the DVD to Record – and then you can watch Christina's butt over and over again, late at night. Mmmm... beautiful!

And now you've done that – give a bit of serious thought to what Mike has to say.

One day you, too, might be locked up in Tussaud's, forced at gunpoint by Blair and Queen 2 to stand still and suffer the pokings and the insults of onlookers for the rest of your days.

Is that what you Britons want? Well – is it? I don't think so. So this is what you gotta do. Write to the chief warder at madame.tussaud@ aol.com and DEMAND that he release those innocent folk RIGHT NOW. And let's hope it's not too late.

Jeez, guys.

Let's kick shit.

The tobacco companies (all run by men) have been extremely successful in convincing the firearms lobby to pacify the car manufacturers by distributing crack cocaine to 132 nuclear plants so that now up to 69% of women between the ages of 28 and 39 are unable to drive their kids to school without inhaling harmful emissions from the ozone layer caused by toxic fumes radiated by President Bush under direct instructions from – yes, you guessed it – the tobacco companies.

So where does that leave the rest of us? Ho-hum. From where I'm standing, guys, it looks like we're drowning in deep doggy-do. And I don't know 'bout you, but deep doggy-do's not something I like to drown in – at least not when there's a Pammy Anderson movie just started on the TV!!!

What in hell's happening to our old folk?

Time was, they'd be plenty of them around. Nice old folk. Good old folk.

Decent old folk. Your grandmom. My grandmom. Everybody's grandmoms. But listen up, guys. As I get older, I've started noticing that something's up.

Yup. The old folk are dying off. My grandmom. Your grandmom. Everybody's grandmoms. They're not there for us anymore.

And, boy, that hurts. That hurts one helluva lot. 'Cos my grandmom's cherry pie was the most lip-smackin' cherry pie that ever there was.

FACT: 97% of people who die in this country are either old or quite old. 97%! I hear you say. Hey, Mike, that's quite a number of old folk to be killed by a single government! So tell me, Mike, what exactly has the Bush administration got against our old folk?

Here's the answer in just one word, boys: they know too much.

FACT: 83% of old people over the age of 75 know 46% more than young people below the age of 25.

Our old folk know too much, and that's why they gotta die. So what can I do about it, Mike? The next time you hear of someone's dear old grandmom falling headlong down the stairs to certain death be sure to check those footprints on the carpet at the top.

Size 10? Well-heeled? Too right. And here's another thing. Take it from me – top bestselling author Michael Moore – it's 91% likely those footprints carry the initials George W. Bush.

Let's get the hell outta here!

Frank McCourt: 'Tos

Oh Jasus. Oh Jasus oh Jasus oh Jasus. Oh Jasus. Will you look at that? asks Dad. I look down at me plate. Oh Jasus he asks, was there ever a child like him for the greed and the gluttony, the gluttony and the greed? And now the others are all staring at me plate, and they'd take a pitchfork to me head out of jealousy if we hadn't sold the pitchfork to old Ma McGubbins to pay for the last season's hay which they needed to feed the donkey to pull the peat to buy another pitchfork to replace the one they'd sold to old Ma McGubbins.

How's he get to have two peas? says Malachy, Oh Jasus, is tis birthday? Dad snatches one of me peas and cuts it in half, snatching half for himself and placing the other half in his top pocket for safekeeping, alongside last year's moth. Malachy caught the moth in his sock and Dad said he'd keep it for our St

Patrick's Day fry-up, moths cook beautiful in batter he said though their wings can prove a mite chewy, it's all that flying they do, Jasus who'd be a moth in this day and age, and aren't I nearly destroyed? Malachy says moths are Protestant, ye've never seen a moth with a rosary, now have you, he says, but Mam says they're good Catholics, and all that flitterfluttering is them making the sign of the cross to the good Lord, is it not.

So I'm cutting me remainin' pea into four and spreading the quarters round the plate to give an impression of quantity when there's a swoosh from the chimney and Great Grandma McCourt emerges covered in soot, her false teeth close behind. She's been out whorin' agin, whispers Alphie. Jasus, how can ye tell, I hiss back. She's suckin' on a cough-drop, says Alphie, They always pay her in cough-drops. But is it not a mortal sin, I ask, Will she not be condemning her soul to eternal damnation?

Not for a cough-drop, snaps Mam, Maybe for a sherbet lemon or two toffees, now shaddup and eat your pea or you won't be getting your mouse-tail for puddin'.

There's a row taking place between Great Grandma McCourt and me Dad. Oh Jasus, says Dad. Don't you Oh Jasus me, says Great Grandma McCourt. I'll Oh Jasus you when I want and where I want, says Dad. Oh Jasus, says Great Grandma McCourt. Don't you Oh Jasus me, says Dad. I'll Oh Jasus you when I want and where I want, says Great Grandma McCourt. Oh Jasus, says Dad.

But just now and at that very moment the St Vincent de Paul Society is staging its annual march-past, horns a-blowin' and hymns a-blarin' preaching love and peace to all mankind. So hearing the cursin' and sensing a mission, they divert into our kitchen, all five of them, let's call it fifty, no two hundred, so's to break up the arguin' and claim two more penitent souls for the Good Lord.

Oh Jasus, say the pair of them as the St Vincent de Pauls break into a grand old Irish hymn:

"The leprechauns are jigging swell
'Pon this moonlit night
The bells 'pon their caps a-jingle
Their dancing shoes all white
As Cuchulain sits 'pon his throne
Lookin' grand and mighty scary
And 'pon his knee – well, bless my soul –
If it ain't the Virgin Mary."

As the chorus flies hither like an angel in the night, Mam arrives in the room wearing the remains of last year's suet pudding while she waits for her dress to dry after the accident with the sheep dip when it sprung a leak while she was gathering the slugs below it for the Sunday stew, but the leak didn't matter, she said, because the last sheep'd run off with Paddy McGarrigey six months before after Paddy had sweet-talked her into marryin' him with the promise of a pen of her own, only the last we heard of the poor sheep was she'd taken to the bottle and was proppin' up the bar in Mulligan's every Friday night with her pint of stout and a chaser by her side sobbin' her heart out that she'd been blinded by love and Paddy'd only wanted her for her wool, bejaysus wouldn't you know the filthy scoundrel. And Mam says, what in the name o' God is goin' on in here, who're all these people tormentin' my eardrums with their carry-on and Dad says, it's the St Vincents, they're reclaimin' our Souls for the Lord, and Mam says, well I trust they've left their fleas outside and Dad says, Fleas, Fleas, what are we waitin' for, woman, take all those St Vincent fleas in hand, train 'em to sing and jig and take 'em to Hollywood – we could be sittin' on a goldmine, woman. So Dad rushes outside but he never manages to catch 'em. Alphie whispers he reckons a flea can spot a loser a mile off.

So now here I am in New York fifty years on and the cheques

are fallin' through the door, muckin' up the carpet and fillin' up the penthouse flat with their dreadful swishin' racket and the investment adviser and the stockbroker are on the phone with their incessant news of more money which I'll somehow have to find a home for and Gregory Peck and Dustin Hoffmann and Robin Williams are sayin' they'll be droppin' round for dinner but the only caviare in the shops is Beluga when everyone knows Sevruga is the best and I'm worryin' that the pastel eggshell blue we chose for the drawing room of our country estate would be better suited to being a little stronger, a little more robust, somethin' closer to navy and sometimes when I look out at the sky and the stars and the moon over Manhattan and I see the lights shimmerin' below I think to myself that this is really no better than the moon that once shone drably over Limerick and nothin' ever seems to be goin' right, what with the follow-up to the tie-in of the book of the movie of the book not goin' well and ten million folk back in Ireland complainin' I've got a tendency to exaggerate and as I stare out at The Statue of Liberty I reflect with a tear dribblin' down my cheek that I am as solitary and cold as that dear sweet stone lady and together we don't stand a fiddler's chance in hell of findin' true comfort and joy, not now that Tiffany's say they're clean out of the diamond chandeliers and yes, the sad news keeps on drizzling like the rain from the sullen clouds, and Jasus, I think it'd destroy me if t'were not for my elfin spark and my indomitable Irish spirit.

Geoffrey Levy Investigates the REAL Virgin Mary

Over the years, the Virgin Mary has gone to desperate lengths to build up a reputation for simplicity and devotion – not to mention sexual purity.

Ordinary, decent, middle-class families the world over look up to her for her legendary care of the less-well-off. In some circles, her name has become a byword for charity. The Pope himself regards her as a saint. But who, close friends are beginning to ask, is the REAL Virgin Mary?

Beneath her carefully-nurtured goody-two-shoes image, who is this woman with the floor-length robes who, friends say, has spent a lifetime battling with a multitude of weight problems?

Strutting the world in her costly designer cloaks – specially designed, experts maintain, to hide the way she see-saws between anorexia and letting herself go – the Virgin has employed every trick in the book to foster her cleaner-than-clean public image.

To be fair, her earning power is undeniable.

In the stark words of one former associate, she works hard and she plays hard. Yet key questions remain about this tactile career woman – questions that continue to baffle even her closest friends and former business associates.

And today these questions look set to rebound, possibly rocking her career and reputation to their very foundations.

So what drives the Virgin Mary?

Friends say that the real Mary is far removed from the saintly image. In fact, I can now reveal, she is a ruthless single parent career woman caught in a tragic love web.

Having grown up in a four-bedroomed luxury home set in two acres – valued at £250,000 in today's terms – the unmarried Mary stuck two fingers up at her hard-working parents by shouting her underage pregnancy from the rooftops.

HE was an ageing out-of-work labourer with no prospects to speak of.

SHE was an underage foreign girl with a baby on the way – and a burning desire to be famous.

Wearing an air of injured innocence – a mask which, former colleagues attest, she ruthlessly employs at all times – Mary managed to persuade the elderly Joseph to make an honest woman of her.

So who exactly was this Joseph – and how could he have fallen for Mary's finely-honed manipulative skills?

Aided, no doubt, by the hard-pressed taxpayer, Joseph delighted in calling himself a carpenter. But – aside from tables and chairs and a full range of bedroom furniture – former friends are unable to recall anything he actually made. One even recalls a "slight tilt" to one of Joseph's much-vaunted tables.

So much for those earlier boasts of fine workmanship.

In truth, Joseph was a tragic old man who cut a pitiful figure in his rootless ethnic circles. But one thing was for sure. Joseph liked living well – even though, as close colleagues confirm, he had a fear of commitment. But, like many men before him, faced with a stunning young pregnant schoolgirl, this decrepit lothario found he just couldn't say no.

To this day, the Virgin Mary dines out on stories of THAT birth.

While many will find it hard to imagine any ordinary, decent mother wishing to regale her friends with tales of giving birth in a sordid cowshed, surrounded by salivating farmyard beasts, close investigation reveals that Mary is, in the words of one former colleague, "fixated with fame – even if it means turning a blind eye to basic hygiene".

Though there is as yet no firm evidence that Mary was at that time on hard drugs, former associates continue to voice their suspicions that the reason she seldom had time for drugs was that she was in the midst of her uphill struggle against weight problems. "If she'd had a mind to take drugs," says one close friend, "then, believe me, drugs are what she'd have taken."

The oddball couple soon made it clear that they had, against the silent majority of concerned parents, decided to call the baby "Jesus".

"It's not a name I'd have chosen for a baby boy," says one former associate. "It makes me shudder to think of the teasing he got in school."

Incredible as it may seem to those who try to give their children a decent start in life, within minutes of the baby's birth Joseph and Mary allowed low-paid farm labourers into the stable to look at the baby.

It is not known whether the pair of them charged the labourers for this facility, but friends confirm that the unmarried couple made no secret of "often being short of a few bob". If the authorities later investigated the matter, their report has never come to light. Whether it was secretly destroyed on the say-so of Mary is a matter for speculation.

Next, it was the turn of the so-called "Three Kings", a shadowy, secretive sect of bachelors in flashy robes, at least one of them an unashamed representative of an ethnic minority. These three unsavoury characters brought small packages into the stable, believed to contain "gold", "frankincense" and "myrrh". Recurrent rumours that they smuggled these substances into the stable intravenously have never been verified.

But one thing is clear. As one child expert puts it, "These are wholly unsuitable gifts for a new-born baby. This is a story that gives widespread cause for concern".

The tragedy of that tragic infant's life – tragic betrayal by a former associate, followed by tragic shame in the courts, and a tragic all-too-public death on the cross, TOPLESS – might have led other mothers to put the brakes on their tireless pursuit of headlines.

But not so the Virgin Mary.

Over subsequent centuries, this ambitious daughter of hard-working parents has never turned up her nose at an opportunity for self-promotion, making ill-judged personal appearances in her signature halo at grottoes and shrines the world over. Perhaps, as friends suggest, it appeals to her massive ego.

She seems to have it all.

Fame. Glamour. Friends in high places.

But will the Virgin Mary ever find true happiness?

Most experts believe it increasingly unlikely. "The last time she appeared at Lourdes," confides one, "I could have sworn I spotted cellulite."

Jordan and Her Guys

Drop-dead gorgeous and so totally to die for. That's what went through my mind when I first set eyes on hunky top people's Chancellor Gordon Brown.

At the time I was going out with TV weathercaster Ian McAskill. What is it with me and weathermen? To give him his due, Ian certainly knew what to do with his hands. But our relationship wasn't going anywhere. For all his talk of sunny spells I never felt he was interested in me for myself. It was time to move on.

I had recently had my bosoms made bigger once more. I needed someone who'd be interested in them for themselves.

———————

It was at a celebrity reception at top club Number 11 Downing Street. From the start, I could tell Chancellor Gordon fancied me something rotten. And believe me the feeling was neutral.

He couldn't take his eyes off them, for starters. Talk about fiscal expansion! I could see he wanted me like mad. But after we had been formally introduced I spelt out my rules. I didn't mind a bit of a kiss and a cuddle, for friendship's sake. But we wasn't to go all the way for a month, or four weeks, whichever was the shortest. And nothing kinky, mind.

As I ran through the rules, that mouth of his hung open like a dog's. To his colleagues, he may have been Chancellor of the Whatever. But to me he was so just a great big bloke.

He may have looked gorgeous with a fantastic body, but Gordon turned out to be a right shit through and through. Frankly, he didn't know how to handle a woman. There I was, dressed to kill in my all-in-one skintight black catsuit, and within a few seconds he had turned to talk to someone else. I can't remember if he even touched my boobs, to be honest.

What is it with me and politicians? Gordon let me down badly. But it would never of worked. Okay, I could of ended up the Chancellor's wife but what's so great about Downing Street? I'd imagined it would be a top-of-the-range luxury mansion. But it was just a normal house, nothing special. I've seen better up Brentwood.

Anyway Gordon was such a sad pathetic loser, with his tongue hanging out and that. I was better off without him. But I'm a survivor. I knew I had to ignore him and keep my dreams alive. Luckily, exactly thirty seconds later who should elbow up to me but one very tasty guy with glasses.

"Hello," he says holding out his hand in the general direction of my famous chest. "I'm top TV historian Dr David Starkey".

———————————

Starkey by name, Starkey by nature. There's nothing I don't know about men and I knew just by looking that underneath that waspish exterior he was panting to rip all my clothes off and take me from behind, on top, me on top, him at right-angles, you name it.

I admit it, I was bowled over by his sunny personality and way with words. What is it with me and historians? Okay, so Simon Schama had let me down badly, and Andy Roberts had shown himself a sick bastard. Sure, I should of been able to see the warning signs, but let's face it I'm a woman who's not half bad-looking, and there was something about them I couldn't get enough of.

David Starkey was talking about the Second World War. "That's terrible news," I said, just to show I had brains as well as boobs. "No one even told me about the first" . He proceeded to tell me about the Western Front and the Battle of the Bulge. I felt he oozed sex appeal and judging by the bulge on his western front Dave felt the same way about me. My eyes had told me Chancellor Gordon was less well-endowed in that department. No wonder he looks so glum.

Before I saw Dave again I had my boobs enlarged specially but as I took off my bra I told him no touching as they was still a bit sore.

But no way, he wouldn't play ball. I didn't see him for dust. I can never forgive him for running away on me like that. Yes, Dr David Starkey let me down badly. He had showed me his nasty side. I should have realised he was only after a quick shag with Jordan the glamour model, and he was never interested in getting to know Katie.

———————

Before I met the Rt Rev George Carey for the very first time, I checked into the clinic to get my boobs made bigger. After all, it's not every day you get to go out with an Archbishop of Canterbury.

I had fancied George for ages. What is it with me and clergymen? He was the strong, silent type. I like that in a bloke. And he always looked drop-dead gorgeous in his cope and mitre.

If he wore anything underneath he wasn't telling – but I was sure as hell determined to find out.

At that time, I was struggling to get over my doomed relationship with top TV quizmaster Bamber Gascoigne (if he could behave like that in front of me, God knows what he was capable of when I wasn't there). In my devastation, I longed for the reassuring touch of George Carey's great big hands playing my body like a piano.

Before I went into his church, I spent hours in front of the mirror making myself look a hundred dollars. I shaved and plucked all the crucial areas – and I mean all (thank you, Gillette!) – and in my wet t-shirt and diamond thong I sat hypnotised below the pulpit as the sun sparkled on his spectacles. So you can imagine my excitement when one of his henchmen touched me on the shoulder and invited me up to the front for a one-on-one.

But when I reached the rail, they went all pervy on me, making me bend my knees and kneel right down on the floor with my hands clasped together across my boobs. What the hell was that all about? No way was I having any of that. "I'm very sorry!" I yelled as I exited that building. "But it doesn't really do it for me."

And that was the last I ever saw of him. He let me down badly, did the Rt Rev George Carey. All right, I had encouraged him, but he hadn't thought twice about making me look a fool.

But's now it's time to move on and put all the heartache behind me, time to let the real Katie Price emerge from the shadow of top glamour model Jordan. To celebrate the new me, and since it's summer, I'm popping into the clinic to add just an inch or two to my boobs. Then I'll be irresistible when I finally get to meet drop-dead gorgeous Sir Nicholas Serota, who I've fancied for ages. What is it with me and art curators?

Sir Edward Heath's
10 Men of the Millennium

GENERAL IDI AMIN

President Amin had a remarkably sensitive eye for Tang Dynasty chinaware. Of course, his country never stopped giving him trouble. But he was a man of great character, and he never allowed his tiresome people to distract him from amassing a most impressive private collection of exquisite vases.

Some now say that Amin was a cannibal, that he enjoyed consuming his enemies. That may be so, but he was also a great gourmet, and would have made sure that they were cooked to the highest possible standard. Nor should we allow these minor details to distract us from his very real charm. Do let's not carp. Historians may argue, with the benefit of hindsight, that I should have taken a leaf from his book and consumed Margaret Thatcher during her disastrous spell as my Secretary of State for Education. But I did not have the necessary implements. Besides, I loathe gristle.

JOSEPH STALIN

Most people now remember Joe for his impressive moustaches, but to me he was also a great leader. He showed enormous character and style, and – unlike the present Conservative leadership – he was never discourteous.

I am well aware that the current generation of historians say he killed a million here, a million there. But that's historians for you. Always trying to play the numbers game. Little do they realise the immense pressure the poor man was under.

Incidentally, Stalin once presented me with some exquisite Waterford crystal, which I bring out for special guests when they come to Sunday luncheon. There was nothing Joseph didn't know about Waterford crystal. A most civilised and impressive world statesman, who would certainly have supported Britain's position in the European community.

KING HENRY VIII

He never allowed himself to get bogged down in the day-to-day detail of his various marriages. Instead, he concentrated on the larger issues. He took firm, decisive action when needed. No one wants to behead a wife, of course they don't. But sometimes it's the only appropriate action.

HAROLD MACMILLAN

Macmillan has been much maligned by the present right-wing generation. But he had enormous style. He used to have his luncheon – a decent claret, oysters, a pheasant or two, cheese, meringues, brandy and coffee, and then a main course – brought in on an individual silver tray with his family coat of arms while he was presiding over our Cabinet meetings. After he had finished, he would turn to the Foreign Secretary, say "Any news from abroad?", slump forward in his chair and take a well-earned nap. Wilson ruined all that, of course. He used to work all around the clock – but to what effect? No one remembers Wilson now, do they? And for all his beavering away, he's still dead!

Didn't do him much good, did it?!!! Meanwhile, I'm still going strong!!! One has to keep a sense of perspective in these matters.

KING HEROD

Sadly, I never met the man, but he offered the people of his country firm leadership when they most needed it. I am fully aware that he had immense difficulties with many in the juvenile sector, but he dealt with them swiftly and decisively. Frankly, you can't go around hiding in bullrushes and expect to get away with it. The poor man had a country to run.

KING ETHELRED

Say what you like about King Ethelred, he was always ready.

GENERAL GALTIERI

At least he had the guts to stand up to her, which is more than one can say for the Bakers and Gummers and Hurds of this world.

And one should never forget that Galtieri was a superb connoisseur of porcelain. He was kind enough to give me a delightful Wedgewood tea-service when I was over on a visit. We have exchanged Christmas cards ever since.

KING RICHARD III

Richard had real charisma, and provided true leadership at a time of crisis. If you don't understand these simple facts, you're a crashing bore.

I know some people hold him responsible for the death of the two Princes in the Tower. But these people simply don't understand the nature of leadership. You can't make an omelette without breaking eggs. Or so my chef tells me. I leave that department to him. But if those Princes were proving a confounded nuisance on all the important issues of the day then they should have expected to be smothered with pillows while they lay sleeping. If they didn't understand that, then they didn't understand anything.

And who let them stay in the Tower in the first place? Richard, of course. He was a most generous host, with a real appreciation of good wine. Those who carp on about his shortcomings are simply proving their own lamentable ignorance of history.

CHAIRMAN MAO TSE TUNG

A most effective chairman of an often uncooperative country. On a personal level, he was immensely thoughtful. He was always pleased to see me. In pride of place on my dinner-table is a delightful sculpture of a peasant worker, constructed with extraordinary skill entirely out of human skin. A most treasured gift. Predictably, the right-wing fringe claim he was a "mass murderer". Utter nonsense. Mao did not murder people. He had them put to death, which is quite a different thing. And if you don't appreciate that, you're dafter than I thought!!

LORD RAGLAN

A first-class military commander, whose achievement at Balaclava was, in hindsight, wholly successful. It suits the stupid right-wing historians of today to claim Raglan was in some way ill-suited for the job. This shows how little they know. The Charge of the Light Brigade was an outstanding success. So much so that they emerged from their experience even lighter. I learnt an awful lot about leadership from Lord Raglan, you know. Without his example to guide me, I honestly don't think I'd have been able to implement my successful three day week.

Salman Rushdie on Bono

Dumas is in gaol, Sirven is in custody, Fujimori has fallen, Clinton is history. In the Middle East, the Two Tribes, as Frankie Goes To Hollywood so ably put it in their ground-breaking, jaw-dropping, chase-cut-to-ing, literally-all-consuming, heart-melting, head-banging song of the same name, Go To War.

The world is at present in one of its perennial hey-what-the-hell's-happening-guys states. And, believe me, it's not a pretty sight. But there's one guy, one god, one good god-guy who's above it all. One guy whose word the world trusts, and in whose trust the world trusts its words. One guy who has our best interests at heart.

And the name of that guy?

Bono.

Bono – Magician, Master, Storyteller, Soothsayer, Wizard, Artist. Troubadour...

Yeah.

I first met Bono backstage on U2's Getting to Grips with World Debt Baby tour at Wembley. I was sitting in a room backstage when he just walked in, *just walked in,* alone and unescorted, just like an ordinary guy, without any of that hey-man-I'm-a-world-megastar step-swagger.

I told him straightaway how much I had deeply appreciated the band's literally superb *Moans for a New Millennium* album, and that I was still in total and absolute knocked-sideways mode having just literally succumbed to the magical complexities of their seminal *Wailing Away* commemorative boxed set.

Then Bono – *Bono!* – and I talked of what was going on in different parts of the world, and what wasn't going on, and how we both wanted to incorporate the whole of what was and what wasn't going on in our novels and CDs in such a way – impactful, insightful, non-pedestrian but above all poeticalish – as to bring the world – the whole of it, and the whole of not-it – literally to its senses.

We rapped into the night, me and Bono – the novelist and the rock star, the rock star and the novelist – the unacknowledged legislators, as T. S. Eliot put it in times-less-turbulent – of the world. And not only the world: *the Universe.*

We discovered we had a lot in common. Bono is a guy of courage and bravery and another synonym who likes to cross frontiers and break down barriers. And I've been crossing frontiers all my life – physical, social, intellectual, artistic borderlines – and I spotted, in Bono and the Edge, the mind-blowingly powerful drummer the Arse and their brilliant bassist Kattomeat an equal hunger – a thirst, even – for the new, for whatever nourishes, for whatever is dangerous and delicious, for whatever can be eaten between meals without ruining the appetite.

An association with U2 is good for one's anecdote stock. Some of these anecdotes are risibly apocryphal and I wish to avail myself of this undoubted opportunity to see them corrected by a free (yeah, right) press. I never, for instance, said that my favourite track on U2's monumental *"Beneath the Drone"* set was *"Weary Is The Song (Homage to Sarajevo)"*. In truth – not a commodity of which the press regrettably has a surfeit of too much, in my view – that particular track was only my second favourite, my favourite being *"Fire of Hope for a New-Style Experience (Module for World Destiny No. 1)"*. But when has the press ever bothered to correct important facts is the question I am now asking?

But some anecdotes that sound apocryphal are – unfortunately! – true. For example, I did meet Van Morrison in Bono's living room and, yes, I did pogo along with the best of them to the new Stewed Prunes CD, and, yes, I have to admit it, I did sit up all night in Bono's 30-bedroom guest lodgings in Killiney – with the odd bottle of Jameson's Irish Whiskey to my credit! – discussing international poverty with internationally-regarded film directors Neil Jordan and Wim Wenders, world-class international supermodel Naomi Campbell, that fine, easily underestimated actor Sylvester Stallone, and U2's consummate horn-player and all-round good guy, Whiskas.

So how did the event happen that I came to write the lyrics for a U2 track? Well, it happened, like many things happen, without being planned. By chance, in other words. Or quite by accident, in other other words. Not deliberately. Without forethought.

In the late 1990s, I was writing a novel about the mythic world of rock 'n' roll (yeah, you better believe it, baby!) called *The Ground Beneath Her Feet.* I was about halfway through this Olympian enterprise when I realised with a start that "feet" rhymed with "meet" and "beat". Over a tortuous, tortured few days, I made the chance discovery that "feel" rhymes with "real", and "true" rhymes with "you".

Yes, I had come up with a ground-breaking lyric of almost mythical intensity which, like all the best rock, had the power to literally move mountains.

I immediately felt that it was my duty as an artist and inveterate front-crosser to send it to Bono. Bono called me. "I've written this melody for your words. I think it might be one of the best things I've ever done." I was both astonished and even more than just astonished – simultaneously astonished and *truly astonished*.

Now U2 have moved beyond their multi-media self-consciousness embrace-debunk post-mythology phase, they are performing more sparely than ever, and their Ennervation Tour is, for me, their most intensely and profoundly impressive yet, reminiscent of their 1989 Portfolio Consolidation tour, but with an even more resonant and haunting undertow of fiscal prudence.

And they're playing my song.

And, at last, the finger of hope reaches out to the world.

The Queen Mother R.I.P.

W.F. DEEDES, Daily Telegraph

It is, in a very real way, the end of an era. Yesterday has gone. Tomorrow, it will be a full two days away. And who knows what the day after will bring? There are seven days in a week, and four weeks in a month, give or take the odd day. Plus ça change.

As we bid this gracious lady adieu, those of us of "a certain age" will recall that she was not always the Queen Mother.

Far from it. Few remember it now, but she was once the Queen, married to King George VI. When her beloved Bertie died, their eldest daughter, Elizabeth, ascended to the throne. Plus ça change.

What would it have been like if Princess Margaret had been the elder?

And what if King George VI had died ten years earlier, leaving the throne open for Queen Margaret? Would we have still won the war? It's easy to forget, but in those far-off days, the fate of this nation hung by a thread. Who knows? Herr Hitler might have considered a Britain reigned over by Queen Margaret – for all her undoubted qualities as a pianist – easy pickings.

We can only speculate. As it is, the Queen Mother lived to a great old age. In her famous hats and coats, always ready with a wave and a smile, she became a very well-known face. Few people, I think, realise quite how fond she was of horse-racing. On the other hand, some say she never got on particularly well with the Duchess of Windsor. Well, these things sometimes happen, even in the best of families. Plus ça change.

CHRISTOPHER HITCHENS, Guardian

Wasn't she marvellous? Well, no, actually, since you ask, she wasn't marvellous at all. In fact, her death marks the end of an anti-democratic era of deference and armchair fascism.

She was billed as the Last Empress of India, but when she kicked off her purpose-built shoes she was only 3 foot 11 inches high. Yet this didn't stop this card-carrying dwarf having the hots for Oswald Mosley, and strutting round the East End arm-in-arm with the old monster screaming anti-semitic abuse through a haze of pink gin.

That's something they don't tell us in the history books. And they also forget to mention her role in the notorious Watergate break-in, taking orders direct from Howard Hunt. And there are still many questions to be answered about exactly what part she played in the Irish Potato Famine, and just how she came to be in Scotland when Pan Am Flight 103 crashed at Lockerbie.

In her private life, she was rarely seen without a fag and a bottle, and spent her rat-arsed days propping up the bar, spouting exaggerated opinions on topics of which she knew very little and cared even less.

Drunk, pampered, louche, burp, I feel a bit queasy actually. Who are you calling louche, you arsehole? Come outside and say that. Whoops, now you've made me spill it all down my trousers.

PETER HITCHENS, Mail on Sunday

Frankly, she is better off out of it. The Queen Mother was born in a great nation confident enough of its fine traditions and rich heritage to teach children the difference between right and wrong by whipping them until they bled.

A proud nation decent enough to eschew such modern atrocities as the "electricated lawn mower" and the "bean bag".

But what sort of nation has she left behind?

A nation in which women are forced to go to work, willy-nilly.

A nation with "television" available at the push of a button.

A nation in which a walk in the countryside can leave one with damp hair and muddy shoes.

A nation in which it is fashionable to pillory old-fashioned virtues like penny-pinching, self-loathing and mutual suspicion.

On the day the Queen Mother died, I happened to be walking down the street. There wasn't a sedan chair to be seen. And – regardless of its proven deterrent effect on young offenders – not a single public execution was on offer.

Instead, motor-cars were going back and forth, forcing people to travel unheard-of distances. Government-run ambulances were carrying innocent people – many strapped to their seats – to their deathbeds. I may even have spotted one driver chewing "gum".

And shops were openly displaying all sorts of unnecessary modern "gadgets" and "household goods". In one window I even saw an electric kettle.

Where were the colourful cut-purses and cheery prostitutes and rapscallions of yesteryear? Nowhere to be seen.

This is a sorry country she leaves behind. A country in which unpleasant groups like the Swinging Blue Jeans and Freddie and the Dreamers holler their obscene songs to lipstick-wearing "Teen-Agers" in darkened clubs where light ale, bubble-gum and Disprin pills are freely passed around.

Let us hang our heads in shame, and say with one voice: "Beg pardon, Ma'am: we, your subjects, have let you down."

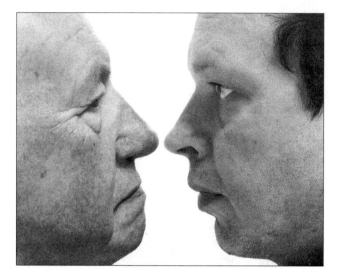

Tom Dixon talks with
Sir Terence Conran

Sir Terence Conran: Before you ask me anything, Tom, there's something I've always wanted to ask you. Tell me, young Tom – as creative director of Habitat, were you hugely influenced by me?

Tom Dixon: Well, not necessarily –

Sir Terence: – you see, I'll never forget the sheer excitement of going to France in the 1950s, when every single person in England was condemned to wear the black bowler hat and walk around on foot, and becoming the first Englishman to discover the beret and the bicycle!

Tom Dixon: That must have been –

Sir Terence: If you'll just let me finish, Tom. So I am immensely proud to have been the very first person to bring the bicycle to Britain. It started with me singlehandedly bicycling along what was then the King's Road, but after less than a year it really caught on, and nowadays, of course, it is commonplace. Nor does anyone wear the bowler hat any more. Though it was a Design Classic in its day, of course.

Tom Dixon: I've often –

Sir Terence: And it's quite extraordinary to think that when I first brought them to Dover, not a soul in this country had seen an onion before. Yet now they are absolutely everywhere. Same with the cushion. I came up with the whole concept of the cushion in the early Sixties. Tremendously exciting times. Until then, everyone had just stayed standing or had sat on exceedingly hard chairs. I still have ordinary decent men and women coming up to me in the street with tears in their eyes and clasping me by the hand and thanking me for the cushion.

Tom Dixon: That's funny, because I remember when I first –

Sir Terence: But there's something I've always wanted to ask you, Tom. Do you think, as so many do, that you owe a vast debt to my whole design concept? I only ask, because before I first invented the whole concept of the roof – or what we then called the Le Roof range – not one single building in the whole of this country had a roof. This meant, of course, that after a spell of rain the goods in all the shops and retail outlets were all tremendously soggy, and the customers would be sniffing and sneezing everywhere because the rain would have been literally pouring onto them in their beds. But I'm immensely proud to say that Le Roof changed all that, which was hugely exciting. And the knife and fork, too –

Tom Dixon: Did you –

Sir Terence: Yes, I invented the knife and fork – Le Knife and Le Fork – back in the marvellous autumn of 1959. Until that time, the typical British dinner party was full of people doing their level best to eat with their hands. This was just about acceptable for a sandwich or even an apple, but as for the stew or the boeuf casserole, well, you can imagine – it was quite simply catastrophic. But that's enough from me about my enormous contribution. As you probably know, I've always been remarkably interested in the young, and what they're thinking. So tell me, Tom – what do you think about my enormous contribution?

Tom Dixon: I've always felt that –

Sir Terence: Of course, in those days, no one had ever even heard of the Chicken Brick. But by June, 1964, the Chicken Brick was quite literally everywhere. There were Chicken Bricks in St Paul's, and all the way along the Strand. The Mall was even decorated with Chicken Bricks for the state visit of the French President. It was a defining moment.

Tom Dixon: By all accounts –

Sir Terence: But one's never been one to sit on one's laurels – and let's never forget that one hadn't even invented laurels back then – so in the September of that year, from my workshop in what was then Bethnal Green, I produced my first range of kitchen furniture. Up until then, no one had ever thought of putting furniture in the kitchen. If you wanted to sit down, you'd have to sit on the floor. The idea took off in an immensely huge way, so by early Spring 1965, I felt confident enough to launch my whole staircase concept onto the market.

Tom Dixon: I've always been –

Sir Terence: People had always had first floors and basements, and so on, but until that moment they'd never been able to get to them. But the staircase revolutionised all that. Yet when we first launched it, retailers came from around the country and said, "Oh, well, the staircase could work in Swinging Chelsea, but it could never happen in Manchester or Birmingham or any one of those dreadfully ordinary little places."

But I remember looking at ordinary working class homes with

two or even three floors still completely unused and thinking, those frankly very ordinary people DESERVE to be able to get to those floors they've frankly never set eyes upon. You see, good design actually has the ability to improve the quality of quite ordinary people's lives. It probably sounds a little pompous to say it, but I've always felt that until I opened Habitat in what was then the Fulham Road no one in London had ever smiled before. And it's hugely humbling to think that I brought such happiness to so many millions of people's lives. And – remember, Tom – this was some months before I happened to design the first shower, or Le Shower. Suddenly, all over Britain, people were clean.

Tom Dixon: I –

Sir Terence: But it was only after I designed the Duvet that sex in this country really took off in a big way. Until then, it had been very much a once-a-year act, usually performed in a very dull grey suit and tie, or long dress, under strict medical supervision. But my whole Duvet concept made sex accessible to everyone – and with my Chicken Brick, you could simmer your Sunday roast at the same time in a different part of the bed, which was truly revolutionary.

But that's enough about me, Tom. I do apologise – I fear I've been far too generous with my advice and reminiscences, and it's time you marvellous young designers had your say, for all your obvious faults! So, tell me, Tom, I imagine it must be hugely disappointing having to follow in the footsteps of such a deservedly influential innovator as my own good self?!

Tom Dixon: Well, in one sense –

Sir Terence: My goodness, is that the time? Must dash! I honestly don't know what we'd all do if I hadn't designed the first wristwatch way back in '66, in what was then South Ken.

George Michael

It's scary, it really is.

Abso-fucking-lutely. Last week, I gave an exclusive interview to *Hello!* magazine. I'm sorry, I'm not going to apologise. I wanted to drag the whole question of Iraq into the political mainstream. I said, we've got to get this one sorted, right? I said, we can't go around killing innocent people, regardless of their sexuality. I said, Bush and Blair have got to do something about all this, they really have.

I was very, very honest and very, very truthful, and very, very courageous.

And you know what was really, really shocking? Not one of the newspapers reported it. Just a silence. A deafening silence. I think they're in serious denial.

Articles about Bush: yes. And Blair: yes. But nothing about George Michael.

Yup. They've effectively silenced the opposition.
And that, my friends, is scary.

It's time someone had the courage to speak out against
everything. I am in the fortunate position that simply by opening
my mouth like this – AAAARRRR! – I am able to save the lives of
literally millions of people. And I don't intend to be silenced.

Let's face it – we are at a watershed in world history. And like
all watersheds, it's full not only of sheds, but of water too. Yup,
this shed is full of water – and we've got to do something. So let's
be brutally honest. You can't store all that water in a shed without
something dreadful happening. First of all, the water could spill
out through the gaps in the walls. Look, I don't pretend to be an
expert in watersheds, or how they're constructed. I'm an artist.
But what I do know is this. If there's too much water in the shed,
then it doesn't matter how many people you've got guarding it,
or trying to plug the holes. That shed is going to burst.

And then we'll all get soaking wet.

Our clothes will be ruined. Our hair will go all flat. And
there's no point even talking about highlights in a situation like
that. It'll all be totally unmanageable.

And that scares the shit out of me.

When 9:11 happened, I was in the middle of writing a major
new song. At that moment, a close friend phoned me and he
said, you've got to switch on the television, you won't believe it.
So I switched on the television and I couldn't believe it. The
whole nightmare was so negative.

My first reaction was – someone out there, and I'm not saying
I know who it is, but someone out there is trying to distract me
from writing my new song.

So I thought to myself, I don't care what happens, they're not
going to stop me. I'm a proud man. I'm a determined man. And

I'm an honest man. Maybe too honest, 'cos then things can get pretty scary. And you know what? I wasn't going to let them silence me. So despite all that negativity, I finished that song. It was very political, very concerned, very real, very brave – and very outspoken. I called it "9:11".

As you know, its chorus went:

> *I want sex*
> *And I want it now*
> *Now, now, now, baby –*
> *Not maybe.*
> *But now. Ow! Ow!*

And the rest is history. The accompanying video showed me dancing topless with a traffic warden in suspenders. It was the only way I knew of bringing the political debate out into the open, and of putting an end to further bloodshed.

When I see Tony Blair answering questions on television, I can tell by the way he looks that he's still mad at me for sticking up for my principles. He's a decent, charming man but ever since I spoke out against the war he's been looking terrified.

But hey, give it a break, I don't want to fight. I'm a writer, not a fighter. Tony's a guy. And I'm a guy. Two guys who happen to be deeply concerned with the state of the world. Between us, we've gotta put our differences behind us and do what we can to sort out the world's problems.

First off, the whole British transport problem.

Look, roads are fine providing there aren't too many vehicles on them at any one time, because then it gets busy and can lead to a traffic jam. And railways are good, too – but you need trains on them to make them work. What does that leave? Boats. Great for the sea, but you can't get far inland in a boat, not unless you find a river going in your direction. And let's not forget aeroplanes – though a lot of ordinary people can't afford one of their own.

By raising the whole Transport issue in public, I'm sticking my neck on the block. But some things are more important than songs, however beautiful. If I can sort out the way we handle all those cars and lorries and whatever on our roads, then I'm prepared to take the flak. Next week, I re-issue my single *Careless Whispers* with major new lyrics. It asks the big question – what are we going to do when there's no more vehicles left to drive? *Carless Whispers* is out Friday.

I'm an intensely private human being, and so's my longtime partner Kenny.

Wherever I go, I'm shocked by the level of negative reaction to my sexuality.

Like, I went through customs at Heathrow the other day, and the customs officer just looked at me as though he didn't want to talk about it. My sexuality's not something I'm ashamed of. Why should I be? If people want to make an issue of it, let them. I've already helped save the Iraqi people, and I don't intend to abandon the fight now.

But sometimes the silence can be deafening. These days, the absence of publicity can be horribly intrusive. Fact – I looked through each one of the Sunday so-called newspapers at the weekend, and there wasn't a single mention of my sexuality – even though my current single is already number 37 in the charts. No pictures of me – even though I totally restyled my hair three days ago.

No pictures of Kenny in his new trousers. And no pictures of any one of the many friendly, caring guys with whom I enjoy occasional sexual relations while pursuing a monogamous relationship with Kenny based on total honesty. So much for a free society! These days, the control the government has over the media is so phenomenal. And not just phenomenal. It's scary.

The Lost Golfing Journals of Sylvia Plath

Saturday 3.45pm: Is this all there is? A ball and a club? A club and a ball? The ball, white, dirty, barely circular, fit for nothing but hitting hitting hitting. The club like the kind of club HE would use to knock the heads off baby chicks before crunching them with his great flat foot splat into the parched ground. Is this all there is? Well, is it?

I join my companions in the changing-room. How to describe them? Let my powers of observation take over, for I must note down all their characteristics, if any, for future use. So here goes: there are three of them, they are human beings on the brink and they are here to take their stab-stabbing stabs at golf, the bastard cruel Nazi sport that stalks the innocent like a centipede in bandages.

I put on my tartan trousers, blood-red and bile-green. I signal for a caddy. There is no caddy my caddy has gone I have no caddy. And he has taken my clubs.

Caddy, I have had to kill you
You took my irons away
Coffin heavy, a bag full of golf
Clubs with a five iron
Missing
And a single tee, red as a virgin's
Period.
Caddy, caddy, you bastard.

4.15pm: It turns out the caddy was waiting for me with my golf
trolley round the front. How to find the words to describe him?
He looks like a man. Young. A young man. He looks like a young
man. Yes, I am a writer!

We walk to the first tee, my legs moving apart then coming
together then moving apart again like a surgeon's blood-soaked
pliers. I take a golf ball from the compartment. It is round, pitted
with dimpled craters, dimpled craters like a leper's buttocks, and,
like a leper's buttocks, meant for hitting. Why do we keep hitting
lepers' buttocks? Through the rain, I imagine myself a leper, my
golf-ball buttocks slammed and swiped by a million satanic
golfers.

I am that leper.

And I feel rage.

4.30pm: Oh what a beautiful game this is, as lovely and ordered
as a full rack of herbs in a well-scrubbed larder before dinner is
served! I have taken a birdy on the first hole, and am now well
ahead of the other women, whose complexions, incidentally,
leave a lot to be desired. No man would be attracted to them!

Every querulous fiber of my body is satiated into a great
glowing peace!

4.45pm: I splutter and gasp, now certain of my doom. Golf grips
me by the throat and chokes me 'til I scream and scream and
scream for mercy. I have done it again, one year in every two I do

it. On the second tee, I use my driver. The ball soars high, high, high into the air before plummeting into the bunker, stubbornly circular and untwitching, like a dead hamster someone has chewed on.

"Bad luck!" shouts one of my companions. I shiver beneath her scorn. I want to wrap my driver round her female neck and strangle strangle strangle her to death, like she would club to death a baby seal, if only she could.

I stand knee-deep in the bunker, swinging, swinging. Sand grains scatter everywhere like another Hiroshima formed of so many bloodthirsty flying rabbits, the long white floppy ears of the sand waggling to and fro like torturing-irons. Sinking deeper as I swing, I curse my caddy.

> *Why? What does it mean?*
> *Why does this golf ball hate me so?*
> *When I try to smash it, it stares back*
> *Undaunted, accusing, like Pilate in Dachau!*
> *Devilish golf-ball! Now you*
> *Crucify me*
> *With your global intransigence.*
> *You would poke at me with a sharpened stick*
> *If only you had the hands for it.*

5.00pm: I am still here, still in the bunker. Above me, the sky looms, glowering blacky blackest black like an electric eel in dark glasses spreadeagled on a blackboard against a black night sky. It is raining mercilessly hard, or would be if it weren't dry and sunny. Scattered showers are expected, if not today, tomorrow. And if not tomorrow, the day after. Or the day after that. I will be drenched like a goldfish. But I will not leave until I have hit my ball. We shall make our home here, here in the bunker. My golf ball is Adolf Hitler, and I his Eva Braun. Oh, caddy!

6.35pm: On the one hundred and eighty-ninth swing, the golf ball rises, slashing the air. Now it is in the rough, the roughest rough of roughs. I push a tee into the ground, like a hypodermic syringe pushing into a corpse. The ball is back, back, back in the air. I have described the golf ball, but how to describe the air? It is virtually invisible, almost see-through, yes – and sparsely furnished. There is not much going on in it: no men, no panthers, no lizards, no nothing. In short, it is *airy*.

The ball teeters on the edge, looking over into the dark centre of the gaping hole. I knock it and it falls, falls, falls. Main fear: I am well below par. I am the prisoner in a cell of my own golfing. But was it like this for Virginia Woolf? When Virginia paraded around her local links did she cry out in pain after bunker trouble on the 2nd hole – or did she take a long, straight drive, ready for a straight birdy on the 3rd? A green seethe of jealousy bursts through the veins. But I bet she was wretched useless rotten with her number five iron the cow.

> *The earthen womb*
> *Cries out for her baby ball back*
> *With my putter, I knock the white round baby*
> *Back into the womb.*
> *The golf ball, shrieking, shrieking,*
> *Hisses into the hole. Then –*
> *Plop.*

7.30pm: Fury jams the gullet. It is grown dark. After 211 shots I am only on the fourth hole. Like an axe, I go for the short cut: I place the ball in my right hand. Then I run around the rest of the course, dropping it in each hole as I pass.

> *Mummy, Mummy,*
> *Why did you not teach me*
> *Better golf? I hate you, Mummy.*
> *Ungodly I hang my head*
> *In shame. No ifs.*
> *No putts.*

The Day I Posed for Lucian Freud

THE RT HON JOHN PRESCOTT:

He comes into my office, right, the office of Leputy Deader, and appertaining to the matter under discretion he sets up his easel and asks me to take off and/or conduct the removalisation of my clothes, up to and including my bubble-dreasted toot and sigh.

Well, hang on I think, I've never met the bloke before, maybe he's one of those predating tory sumo hexuals we read so much about. So I keeps on my vest and my Y-fronts, and I say "I'll go this far but no further. Now where do you want me sat?" He says he wants me splayed out on the office desk with a rose out me arsehole and a ballpoint out me left ear. "Out!" I say, pointing to the door and pressing the button for Security. If this is Modern Art, you know where you can shove it. Frankly, I've never been so insultivated in all my dawn bays.

JILLY COOPER:

As Lucian wielded his gi-normous brush in his big strong hairy masculine hands, Jilly lay back on the expensive couch, purchased five years ago in a moment of sheer madness from Heal's store in London's fashionable Tottenham Court Road, and positively quivered with excitement. It seemed as though her whole body was aching with the desire to be painted by this Casanova of the canvas. How she wished he would fling off his beret, strip off his smock and ride her like a red rosette-winner in a top people's gymkhana.

"There's no SMOCK without fire," she giggled, punningly. She could see he was about to collapse in hoots of laughter, so she added, "I hope this will be a 'STILL LIFE', Lucian! Because there's certainly STILL some LIFE left in me!!!!"

At that moment, Lucian's moody gaze seemed to erupt in an explosion of merriment. Golly, he looked so deliciously sexy when he giggled, thought Jilly. A tear came into her eye. In a certain light, he reminded her of her gorgeous, faithful and utterly utterly darling three-legged mutt, Bubbles, whom she had had to have put down at the end of last year, in time for Christmas. Bubbles and Lucian both had that look in their eyes, that playful glint that seemed to say, "I'm lovely and I'm sexy and I'm wholly irresistible!" The only difference was that Lucian didn't have a tail to wag around.

Or did he?

SIR TIM RICE:

> *I'd never get into a feud*
> *With Lucian Freud!*
> *That would be very rude*
> *And not at all good!*

THE RT REVEREND GEORGE CAREY:

What exactly do we MEAN when we say that this or that artist is going to "paint our portrait"? This is the question I put to the painter Lucian Freud as I undressed for him and sat on a bar stool with one foot in the air for my official retiring portrait as "ArchB of C" the other day.

Lucian can't have heard me, because he just stood there with a very concentrated expression on his face. So I tried my level best to answer the question for him. "I suppose what we really mean, correct me if I'm wrong," I said, "is that he – or she, because let's not forget there are some tremendously able women artists in operation at the present time – is going to try to put down their impressions of us as 'human beings' on a canvas, using paints and brushes rather than just words.

"It's all about our old friend 'communication'. That's the name of this particular game, wouldn't you agree, Lucian?"

Oddly enough, he didn't reply. He just marched up to me and re-adjusted my mitre, pulling it over my eyes.

"I've always thought Jesus was a prime mover in the communication game," I said, wondering where I was. "In fact I sometimes think he'd be playing for Man U. if he were alive today – which of course he is, in ways we can't hope to fully understand. Tell me, which team do you support, Lucian? I'm a huge Gunners fan, myself!"

Lucian replied with a lovely simple gesture which will remain with me for many a long while yet. Very gently and with great tenderness, he placed a lovely woolly sock in my mouth. It was to me a very warm, very Christian gesture, a reminder that there is a world beyond words. But what exactly do we MEAN by "words"?

Roy Jenkins:
12 Tube Stations

HAINAULT

Hainault is, one might almost suggest, the most oxymoronic of tube stations, being on the Central Line, but very far from central. East of Woodford, yet due south of Grange Hill, it is not a station with which I would claim an instinctive and intimate relationship, rather one which I would say has always greeted me most warmly, offering to carry my bag, whilst stopping short, as it were, of asking me in for a bottle of halfway-decent claret, accompanied by a modest yet inarguably varied selection of choice olives.

I have, I confess, visited Hainault barely once in 80 years. In fact, to be brutally frank, I have never found cause to visit it at all, preferring, when I have the time, to travel by what the French rejoice in calling the "limousine". But I am most reliably informed that many far from disagreeable people avail themselves of the Hainault stop on a daily basis, and I have little doubt the pleasures it affords them are not only paradoxical but also highly convivial.

TOTTERIDGE AND WHETSTONE

I first saw Totteridge and Whetstone when I was, I fancy, but fifteen years of age. I cannot claim, in all honesty, ever to have been back. He would be a saint who could place it among the first rank of London underground stations, and I make no claim to sanctity, though over the years I have enjoyed close, though seldom intimate, acquaintance with no fewer than six Popes and seventeen Cardinals. I was never a Cardinal myself, though I cannot claim this omission causes me a very great deal of regret. In the late 1950s, I was for a short while Archbishop of Verona, but, for all its splendid sartorial opportunities, I found the post in the main tiresome, and communication with the Lord Almighty for the most part haphazard and tiresomely one-way.

Nevertheless, Totteridge and Whetstone has remained vivid in my mind. I make no claim for it as a rival to, say, the sheer magnificence of Place Vendome in Paris, or, for that matter, the extravagant Neo-Gothic of the Plaza de Colon in Madrid. It is set, a trifle clumsily, in surroundings that are not, one must confess, greatly conducive to the pleasures of the table or, indeed, the amenities of social intercourse. Neither High Barnet, its more northerly neighbour, on the far from undistinguished Northern Line, nor Woodside Park, its somewhat less trumpeted southerly companion, offer overwhelming reasons for stopping. But Totteridge and Whetstone has always possessed for me a certain creaky charm, albeit a charm sadly insufficient to draw one back more than once every sixty years.

WARREN STREET

It was in the warm glow of an afternoon in late September that I first set eyes on Warren Street underground station. It is not, perhaps, a first-rate station, still less a second-rate station, but as the lower third-rate stations go, I have always considered it ranks really rather high, if not at the very top, then quite near the upper-middle.

It was during my time, not entirely wasted, as Minister for Transport that I found myself passing through Warren Street. The train itself was less luxurious than utilitarian. In terms of comfort it could never, I think, compare with the Orient Express or, for scenery, with the Trans-Siberian Express, both of them very considerable trains. But it possessed features rarely found in some of the more ostentatiously feted vehicles, as I pointed out to Giscard d'Estaing and Pierre Trudeau, who were journeying with me at the time.

"That's a really rather charming cushion over there," I remarked to Pierre, pointing to a soft yellow item on the banquette opposite. "If not exactly a first rate cushion, then certainly high among the lower seconds." At this point, Pierre, a man with an adventurous, if not perhaps always sagacious, turn of mind, stood up and walked over to the cushion in question. "This is, I fear, no cushion," he said, sniffing it with the instinctive delicacy of a French-born Canadian. "It is a pool of vomit."

Up to that point, I had never, I confess, come across quite such a pool of vomit on the banquette of a major underground railway train. For this reason, I was drawn to study it more closely. Rather to my regret, I found it somewhat less impressive, both in hue and texture, than a pool of vomit most memorably produced by George Brown outside the Savoy Hotel in the cold winter of '66 after a lengthy repast during which he, as Foreign Secretary, had been attempting to steer us through delicate trade negotiations with the Eastern Bloc.

WEST KENSINGTON

West Kensington is one of the most rewarding, if under-appreciated, tube stations on the entire District Line (with the notable exception of Turnham Green, which rivals it in sophistication and, to my mind, surpasses it in *comfort cossu*).

I first visited West Kensington in the spring of 1983. I was, by that time, both General Secretary of the World Trade Federation and Chairman of the World Bank, as well as President of the European Commission, three posts which, I am happy to relate, left one ample time to get on with more useful and more pleasurable, if not necessarily more remunerative, pastimes.

It was not my wish to embarrass the far from disagreeable staff of the District Line by landing on them "out of the blue", as it were. They would not, I surmised, be used to dealing with a man not unblessed with my undoubted lack of indistinction, so with due forethought I had a message posted in advance that the President of the European Commission, etcetera, etcetera, would be arriving at such-and-such an hour on such-and-such a day, giving them plenty of time to lay out the red carpet and so forth.

As I remember it, I had just stepped onto the "down" escalator when the red carpet they had earlier laid upon it began to "ruck up' at the bottom, causing myself and my honoured guests – who included the Lord Provost of Glasgow, Sir Isaiah Berlin, The Duke of Westminster and Dame Anna Neagle – to hurtle head-over-heels down forty-odd steps or more. An unfortunate occurrence, perhaps, but what it lacked in dignity it more than made up for in exhilaration, so we immediately climbed the stairs and did it all over again.

Sara Cox

SARA: Y'know when you got this great big sort of bogey thingy up your nostraw and you like widdle it around with your finger but it somehow still won't wosser word, you know, get out? Joonota mean? Right, so you got this great big sort of bogey thingy up your nostraw and you're like going ravin' mad like tryin' to like you know widdle it around with your finger and gerrit out, right, joonota mean? Well, tha happened to me last night, it did, honest, like I was just sittin' there, trying to what's the word, dislodge, yeah, dislodge this bogey but would it come out? No, it wouldn't, I'm tellin' you it wouldn't!!!!!!! Wooh! Mad!

It's 8.46 and comin' up we got the results of an IGSLUSIF interview with Robbie, cwor, don't half fancy Robbie, eh, girls, he ain't half sexeh, wouldn't mind findin' what he's hiding up his trousers, eh, girls, joonota mean? Wooh! ONE LIFE ONE STATION THE RADIO ONE BREAKFAST SHOW.

It's like 8.48 and there's a six-mile tailback on the A1039 outside Leicester so let's like hear the news headlines from one guy who's got a lot going on in his trousers – Matt.

MATT: It's boom time all round as President Bush starts dropping his bombs on Saddam Hussein, Posh and Becks say no to war, another schoolgirl is murdered – and a chance to win VIP tickets and mix with top celebs as J. Lo struts her stuff at the UK Premiere of her latest movie. ONE LIFE ONE STATION THE UK'S URFISHL NUMBER ONE – RADIO ONE.

SARA: Like yesterday I had this great big massive wosser word, yeah, need, I had this great big like massive need to have a woddya call it, yeah – POO, right? But I wasn't at home, I was stuck in like this tailback on the M1 I think it was, and I so I'm going, like, I really like need to have this great big massive poo, but where'm I gonna do it, joonota mean? Talk about clenchin' the old buttocks, right?! Anyweh, luckily I made it back just in time and had my poo, like gwah, the relief, you can't belieeeve it, so this got me thinking, right, I want to hear from any of you who've had a similar last minute poo experience, joonota mean? Ahm not necessarily talking 'bout pooin' in your pants, though we must have all done that in our time, joonota mean? But if you got a great poo story that happened to you or your mates then mail me on wwwdotbbcdotcodotukforwardslashradio1 and I'll read out your all-time best poo stories, shoo be great.

Dja watch Fooballer Swives last night, dja? Mandy from Hartlepool just e-mailed to say she don't half fancy that Jason, and she's like pretty sure he's got the biggest willy of the lot of em judging by that BULGE, joonota mean? So I was watching Fooballer Swives last night eating prawn flavour Skips well, to be honest, they weren't prawn flavour Skips they were like Marks and Spencer own-brand prawn flavour skips but like to you and me they were Skips 'cos I know a Skip when I see one. Just got an e-mail from Dave in Totnes saying he once had a poo in a shower at his auntie's house, thanks for that, Dave, and another from Sue from Guildford who goes I once had a poo on the verge of the M4 outside Newbury and like it was SO EMBARRASSING, right, 'cos this lorry driver sticks his head out of his lorry and sees her havin' a poo right there on the verge, that's the M4 outside Newbury, this massive poo, right? Gray story, Sue!

Teya wha', this Iraq business right, like, this whole Iraq thing, joonota mean, like last night I'm like watching the news with Trevor McDonald, sexy guy, Trev, crackin', and I'm like watching the news about the Iraq thing, and I'm thinkin' now, the big debate comes down to this: if I had to, would I rather snog George Bush or Saddam Hoodjamaflip? Tricky one. I mean, like, I'd probably rather go clubbin' with Saddam, 'cos, like he's got that wosser word that's right moustache and everything and he looks kind of mean and broodeh, but for a serious snog I'm not so sure I might not go for George Bush he's got skin like a baby's bum and I bet he'd be up for a bitta toe-suckin'! E-mail uz now with your opinion on the big issue – whoodja wanna snog most, Bush or Saddam? Now let's go to Matt for an update of the latest world news wotsit from Radio 1!

MATT: Millions perish as nuclear bomb blows top country to smithereens – traffic build-up due to overturned lorry on the A12 outside Chelmsford – the tortoise who can't stop farting – and Mel C says no to the Spice Girls! All this and more coming up on Newsbeat.

SARA: Wossat about fartin', Matt, dja say summat about fartin'?

MATT: There's a tortoise who can't stop farting, Sara.

SARA: A tortoise who can't stop fartin'. Blimey! Cheeky sod! Just think – a tortoise who can't stop fartin'. Wodya say it was, Matt?

MATT: A tortoise who can't stop farting, Sara!

SARA: Sounds like yours truleh after I've had like all the Baked

Beans, joonota mean?!!! Come on you lot out there, I bet you got some gray fartin' stories for us – e-mail them in and we'll give the winner a VIP night out at Stringfellows where you'll get to mix with all the real mega celebs, right. Wooh!

Dja see EastEnders then last night dja, I mean like I was going like, wossis – that lad's gorra nice bum on him, wouldn't mind a birrava nibble on that, joonota mean? E-mail just in from Kate from Birmingham who says I always fart after a hot curry and so does my boyfriend Tim and another from Greg from Wisbech who goes he was once like caught short on the B3136 outside Shepton Mallet and he found himself havin' to do a poo into a Coke can, wooh, too much information, Greg, then there's another from Trev from Greenock in Scotland, och aye the noo, who says just 'cos a nuclear bomb's gone and bin dropped on a foreign country no one's ever 'eard of that's no reason not to boogy along to Toad Rappaz incorporating DJ Stunted who he says are like the greatest band that's ever bin of all time in the world ever and they're playing a gig tomorrow night at the Empire in Glasgow, hoots mon there's a moos in the hoos, joonota mean? It's comin' up to 8.55 and there's still an hour to go on Coxie's Breakfast on wosser word Radio 1.

Will Self

I myself – or, rather, the "I" that is me, or was me at that perfidious axiom in the Newtonian time/space continuum that occurred at just that moment, or instant, when I began, or started, this sentence, this collection of inter-related words or phrases – I myself grew up with absolutely no idea, or conception, of what it meant to be a man, or even to be masculine.

My father, it became clear, or evident, as I grew up, or got older, was a man – in very much the same way as my mother, as I was later to discover, was a woman – *womo sapiens*. A man: a woman. The former wore trousers, the latter dresses. Theirs was, spied through the catastrophicatory prism of the outside world, what would then have been called, or termed, a conventional marriage.

Mired in respectability, my father never talked about

possessing a penis, and all that implied. Perchance he was in what Hegel, my capable if deceased lab-assistant in advanced studies in the exigencies of existence, would have termed a state of denial. Yet I now realise, or understand, that he in all likelihood employed his penis for all sorts of things – for scooping the last few snot-like albuminously laden dribbles from the nether of a lightly boiled egg, or as a convenient draught-excluder on preternaturally windy nocturnes, or as a handy putter on the golfing greens to which he was less a visitor than an attachment – to which he was too churlish, or embarrassed, to confess.

Like an estate-owning wildebeest, my father occupied, or inhabited, vast reserves of self-centredness. Standing by and watching him as he lay there putrefying on his deathbed I was flabbergasted that he didn't once ask after my own health, which, at that time, was commendably tip-top, and worthy of lengthy discussion. Instead, ever the solipsist, he self-pitying writhed and gasped, never even bothering to keep still while I noted down the peculiar colour – mauve, tinted with the pea-green of a laburnum soaked in urine – of his toes, for use in my acclaimed fifth novel, a set of inter-related narratives termino-execroballetically examining the whole nature of mortality through the eyes of a transsexual goldfish with a compulsive eating disorder and an obsession, or mania, for Descartes.

When finally my father had the grace to turn the volume of his writhings and gaspings to a notional zero on an imagined control-knobule, I generously submerged any feelings of blame or repugnance I might have been expected to foster, or incubate, in order to read to him, with lovingly-timed emphases, from my last book, a profoundly unnerving and searingly acute study of the whole death thing. It was when I was vocally hovering over the important fifth sentence in the nineteenth paragraph that a whitecoated nurse broke, or shattered, the sequentiality of my narrative by pushing past me to put her fingers and thumb to my father's wholly nondescript bourgeois wrist in order to feel his typically slack pulse.

"I am sorry to tell you this," she said, naturalistically, "but your father passed away some time ago."

I sat there dumbfounded, an air of cosmic bewilderment entering my skull and setting up home there, ready to emerge, years later, in a series of cutting-edge masterpieces. Dead – just when he should have been listening to me reading from a work-in-progress! This behaviour was all too typical, or characteristic. Not only had my father died without bothering to let me know – his cackhandedness in arrangements involving others was always astonishing – but he had passed on without even signalling his applause for the ingenuity, or complexity, of my new narrative. It was with near pity that I left the hospital, for his all-embracing solipsism had, in these last few moments of his life, deprived him of the chance to enjoy a one-to-one personal reading by his soon-to-be justly-celebrated son.

It's only this that motivates me to write about him at all: this vexed question of masculinity, of what it is to be a man. An unutterably grey nimbus of brutality surrounded my parents. They fought to the death, brandishing decency, the nuclear weapon of the suburban bourgeoisie. On the crap terrace of our suburban semi, my mother would coldheartedly ask my father how his day had been. Shielding the blow, he would reply, viciously, that it had been fine – and with a final savage swipe he would then tell her to put her legs up, before threatening her with a "nice" cup of tea. The two of them were a schizophrenic hermaphrodite, their marriage a screaming Procrustes, always stretched to breaking point – and beyond. I once overheard my mother say, "How about a nice biscuit then, dear?" It was a dubiously interrogatory phrase designed to force upon the prostrate victim an all-out assault, or attack, that could be met only with the tiny porous shit-brown shield of the absent Hobnob. When my father replied, "Mmm... lovely", I knew then that he had allowed his manhood to wither into a nothingness as weary, diminished and yet somehow sublimely totemic as a small mollusc stamped upon by an elephant before being subdivided with a pair of compasses by an aberrant algebraitician who is nursing a rare neurotic compulsive disorder that forces him to make things very small, or minuscule, indeed.

So at no point did my parents teach me how to be a man, or what a man was. As an artist, I find myself bedevilled, or bevilled, when it comes to the consideration of wherein my manhood really inheres. As a writer, I embody the caesura in which Western male society, or civilisation, now finds itself: civilisation, or society, is, to a very real extent, placed somewhere between its fifth novel and second book of short stories, widely-reviewed and, occasionally appearing with a wry half-smile on television, but somehow lacking in depth, or deepness.

Is this all there is?

"What is a man, here in the 21st century?" I asked my friend, the novelist J.G. Ballard. "A man," he replied, "is the stain of pus on a discarded band-aid, the last nasal hair as it disappears down the plug-hole." Myself, I would take a less sentimental view. I sometimes feel myself to be plunging towards watery extinction, weighted down with the ballast of my own priapic masculinity, yet I cannot assay it, though I must continue to try, for I know not what it is, this I, this myself, this me me me me me me me me

Mo Mowlam

It soon became evident I wasn't like other politicians. Word got around that I was big-hearted and warm and enjoyed a joke. That I was genuinely nice, disarmingly honest and wholly genuine. And that without mentioning names (smarmy Mandelson, two-faced Blair, Machiavellian Campbell, moody Brown, pompous Irvine) – unlike the others, I was not inclined to criticise colleagues behind their backs.

I was easily the most popular Cabinet Minister in the New Labour Government – and it was beginning to make my stuffy colleagues jealous. I was just too honest and upfront for my own good. "If I could just say a word, Tony, before this meeting gets underway," I'd say in Cabinet, giving Jack Straw a lovely, lovely hug. "Just something I think you all ought to know. On the way here today, a really smashing old lady came up to me, bless her, and said, 'We love you, Mo! You're better than the lot of 'em! How long will we have to wait before you're Prime Minister, then?!'

"I just thought you'd want to know. I knew you'd be happy for me! Thanks, guys!"

Me and my big mouth! Call me innocent, call me too good for this world or whatever, but I had reckoned without their seething jealousy. I soon began to feel desperately isolated. Everyone in the Cabinet was trying their hardest to live up to my professionalism – but sadly I was by far the most popular with the public. And that was when the whispers began. "Whisper whisper whisper." This was what I overheard when I entered Downing Street early one morning hoping to catch up on my mammoth post-bag of fan letters before Cabinet. Tony was huddled up with Gordon and a senior official from the Treasury. "Whisper whisper whisper." "Let us in on the secret, guys!" I joked. Frankly, they didn't know where to look. You see, I could tell that under the guise of "checking" through the "Treasury figures" they were really talking about Yours Truly. Generously, I attempted to set them at their ease by rising above it all. "It's really great you guys are working so hard on your sums!" I said, warmly, "And I think it's really unfair that you backroom boys with your pocket calculators remain under-appreciated by the general public, while I continue to soar ahead in the opinion polls!"

This was the point when my relationship with Tony began to get rocky.

Looking back, he had long nursed resentment of my personal warmth and spontaneity.

During one particularly boring Cabinet, when poor old Gordon was droning on, bless him, about the balance of payment figures (yawn! yawn!) I felt I would be better employed keeping everyone around the table happy by supplying them with food and drink. So I reached below the Cabinet table for my tupperware and thermos, and started spreading the ready-sliced with generous dollops of Hartley's New Jam.

"I'm envisaging a broad-based two and a half percent overall rise over a three-year period, but with a contingency plan if –" droned Gordon.

"Jam sandwich, anyone? Choccy biccy?" I said, setting them all at their ease, "Go on, Jack, be a devil – you could do with a bit of feeding up!"

At this point, Gordon (sadly, many of his friends find him a difficult, moody man, and hard to get to know) attempted to interrupt. He had long nursed the ambition to take over from Tony as PM. It must have been very hard watching me sailing ahead of him so effortlessly. But I was determined not to budge from my key role of making everyone happy by keeping up the dialogue. So as he sat there stubbornly blahing on about fiscal policy, I put up my hand and proposed an un-stuffy sing-song. "Anyone know that one off the first Fairport Convention album?" I said.

I am famously sensitive to the little quirks and foibles of other human beings (for my sins!). Was it just me or, even as I was hard at work tuning up my guitar, did I sense a mean-spirited atmosphere springing up around that Cabinet table? I might have expected better of my colleagues, who not so long ago had marched alongside me in the fight for freedom and justice. I was certainly saddened when no-one saw fit to join in, and when I looked up to see Tony's fingers firmly lodged in his ears, I began to wonder whether he was quite up to the job.

I often wonder how big a part my great big hugs played in bringing peace to Northern Ireland.

Northern Ireland is a distant country, full of warm and lovely Irish people who grew to worship me when I ruled over them. "Just call me Mo," I would tell them – and they adored me for it. There were, of course, the inevitable criticisms from the hardened, embittered, intransigent Loyalist community that I favoured the Republican cause. Nothing could have been further from the truth. It was nothing personal, but I just didn't particularly like the so-called Loyalists, and didn't see why they should always refuse to play ball. After all, as I told Trimble, their links with the real mainland British were pretty tenuous, so – dur! – why were they so keen to cling on?

When all else fails, a hug works wonders. I ended our first series of crisis talks by bringing all sides together – not only Trimble and Paisley but reasonable men like Gerry and Martin – put John Lennon's "Imagine" on the CD and called for "one great big huggy-hug". Don't blame me if half of them walked out in a stomp! Talk about babyish!

Tony called me in. I was totally upfront. I asked him to sit down and tell me how best he thought he could serve the New Labour government. He said he thought I should move from Northern Ireland to Health or Education. I told him that I felt the best way to serve my country was to do all three, with the additional option of taking over the Foreign Office once poor Robin Cook, bless him, had been warmly eased out. This was just the sort of broad-based vision for the future that had originally inspired me to fight the cause of New Labour. But it was made clear to me that Tony had lost sight of the vision. What I think was so difficult for everyone to deal with was Tony's attitude that he always knows best, and the way he stubbornly continues to think of himself as Prime Minister.

Alan Watkins

There has been disagreement in recent years over the etymological derivation and correct spelling of the word "Burp". Historians may care to note the correct version, which follows in the next paragraph.

Contrary to the version put about by the formidable Mr Roy Spangle in his admirable Fleet Street memoir, "17 Years a Deputy Home Affairs Correspondent for Beaverbrook", now out of print, the term "Burp" was in fact coined by Mr Peter ("Pete") Greenwood, the formidable chief sub-editor on the old Daily Sketch from 1951-67.

Mr Greenwood was a man of medium height, who wore dark brown shoes of a conventional styling.

The story goes that, three-quarters of the way through his preferred breakfast tipple, a triple brandy-and-claret with malt whisky chaser, in El Vino in late October 1965, Mr Greenwood was offered another, to which he replied with this memorable: "Burp!"

Prior to that occasion, the traditional eructation had been "Barf" (sometimes rendered "Barph") or "Blurrgh" (often incorrectly pronounced with a silent "g"). So when Greenwood said "Burp!", and then repeated it three seconds later – "Burp!", or possibly "Burrp!" – three of us reached for our notebooks to record this historic event.

The following year, I heard the expression employed repeatedly at the Labour Party Conference, and again seven weeks later while partaking of luncheon at the Gay Hussar with Mr Tom Driberg, a formidable politician distinguished by his very slightly larger-than-average height. Today, "burp" has become the standard utterance. "Barf" and "Blurrgh" have all but disappeared, though they are still given an occasional run around the block by Sir Peregrine Worsthorne. It is, as Mr Macmillan remarked in June 1954, as well to know these things.

The late Mr John Junor was a redoubtable figure. "Never trust a horse that winks" was a phrase he would intone over a convivial glass of Teacher's whisky (2/6, or five shillings for a double, cheaper before 6.00pm and on Sundays) in El Vino. "A pigeon should not be eaten if its wings are still flapping" was another.

A formidable man of average height, he was given to wearing a leather belt with his trousers. It was rumoured that this was to keep them up. I once set eyes upon the soles of his shoes. To my untutored eye, they looked perfectly normal. I was to discover later that this was indeed what they were. Though eccentric in other areas, he had, it appeared, no unusual tastes in shoes.

The third best Junor-and-household-flowers story is invariably misreported. The story goes like this. He once took me to one side, clasped my shoulder and advised me to buy tulips. "Only poofs like daffodils," he remarked. This amusing story is often recounted inaccurately, with dahlias instead of daffodils.

The position of the Liberal Democratic Party – often wrongly referred to as the Liberal Democrat Party – in twenty-one years' time is a matter of conjecture.

I make no predictions. But if, as seems likely, Mr Charles Kennedy – wrongly believed to be a nephew of the President Kennedy – sees his party lose seats at the next General Election, then in the following election, which will be held in October, or possibly September, 2005, he will have a hard job keeping his head above water.

By May 2009, Mr Kennedy may find himself occupying a position similar to that of Mr Leonard Hutchings in the historic autumn of 1923. By June 2010 he will be lucky to fare much better than Mr Arnold Blackstone-Leigh in the August and subsequent September of 1937.

However, the signs are that in the snap General Election of the first two weeks of November 2012, the Lib Dems will enjoy a change in its fortunes, gaining perhaps 29 or 30 parliamentary seats, some of them marginal. This will put them in good stead for the General Election of Spring 2016, possibly under a new leader. They will then return to their present healthy position when the polls close in mid-March 2021, allowing them to enter the May 2025 election with renewed confidence. This would put them in a good position to push through some sort of Proportional Representation, partially amended on the Burroughs/ Burleigh 1931 model, in time for the subsequent election in June 2024. But politics is a notoriously chancy business; I make no predictions.

Mr Adolf Hitler was a formidable politician of average height, clean-shaven but for a postage-stamp moustache placed with commendable exactitude in the centre of that area between his nose and his top lip.

Though he was admired by many, and in addition possessed an admirable working knowledge of the German language, I never warmed to him. Perhaps I sensed a reckless side to him, for I was later to hear that he had wreaked havoc in his home country and abroad.

He was a teetotaller, with non-descript elbows. It was said of him that he had a bit of a temper, a trait he undoubtedly shared with Mr J. Seaforth-Smedley, the unfortunate Conservative and Unionist Party candidate in the infamous 1932 Stockport North by-election.

November 1989 proved a redoubtable month. Mr Jack Huggins, the Observer's chief sub-editor, left for The Sunday Express, to be replaced by the formidable Mr Patrick "Pat" Parkins, a man of medium height, who was to appoint none other than Mr Trevor Banks as his deputy. This left a gap on the Sports Desk, filled by Mr Clive Astley. Mr Astley had well-brushed hair and pronounced the word "gin" to rhyme with "din", a common mistake.

Halfway through this era of historic and tumultuous change, the news came through that the Berlin Wall had fallen, thus handing me on a plate my subject for that week. My 1257-word piece that Sunday reminded readers that in 1951 Mr Hartley-Crossland's garden wall on the North East side of marginal Beaminster constituency had also fallen. There had been no repercussions worth worrying about. As the late J.P. Stopes once remarked to me over a glass of formidable Brouilly, "It's never worth getting over-excited. You look as though you could do with a top-up, Alan."

Tony Parsons

Make no bones about it.

Saddam Hussein is a thoroughly nasty piece of work.

A mass-murderer. A slimebag.

And a foreigner to boot.

Not the kind of bloke I'd ever want to share a natter with over a pint and a packet of Cheesy Footballs down The Old Red Lion.

Come to think of it, whatever happened to Cheesy Footballs?

And whatever happened to The Old Red Lion?

Gone, but not forgotten.

Just like Saddam. And you know what?

Saddam deserves what's coming to him.

With brass knobs and thumbscrews on.

You know what folk down my street are all asking?

I'll tell you.

They're asking this – how does Saddam compare with our own right royal figurehead, the late Queen Mum?

To me, there's no comparison.

Don't kid yourself, Saddam.

You never took the trouble to visit the bombed-out East End during historic World War II.

You never kept us smiling through the toughest times, radiant and well-turned-out, a symbol of all that was once Great about Britain.

Yes. It's official.

The British people loved the warm-hearted Queen Mum.

And they don't give a fig for a tosser like Saddam.

But fair's fair. I admire the Queen Mum. But make no mistake.

Given the choice, it's Rod Stewart's lovely lady the gorgeous Penny Lancaster we'd all give a good seeing-to.

The girl's got everything.

Great legs. Terrific tits. A bubbly personality. Get-up-and-go. The lot.

Which makes me wonder.

If Tony Blair really wants to show the world what we Brits are capable of, why can't he hitch up with someone more like Penny Lancaster?

Take it from me. Penny would look a million dollars leaping up those White House steps to greet President George W. Bush in a thong.

Instead, what does Blair do?

The guy skulks around with a middle-aged mother-of-four who wastes her spare time yacking in court, if you can believe it, and couldn't lap-dance to save her life.

Okay, so Penny's spoken for. Rod's not likely to give her up without a fight, and who can blame him?

But Jordan's still single. And she's one hot babe. Any red-blooded bloke would be proud to have her on his arm.

And not only on his arm, mate.

So prove you're a man, Tony.

Present Cherie with her marching orders. Tell her to take the sprogs with her.

Install Jordan in Downing Street by Spring.

And you'll have earned my vote, any day.

I've just been reading the new novel by Gabriel Garcia Marquez.

And it's blown my mind.

It makes that tired old slapper Victoria Beckham look like a total has-been.

Gabriel Garcia can do everything. Words. Sentences. Paragraphs.

Even whole chapters.

And what can Victoria Beckham do?

In a word: Sod All.

Can she sing? No.

Can she dance? No.

Can she fill up space? No.

Or at least not much.

But I won't hear a word against her husband, footballer David.

Now, there's a bloke who's handy with a football.

It's high time the toffee-nosed high-ups in the Football Association made him Captain of England.

And then it'll be, Arise, Sir Beckham!

But not you, Mrs B – you can bloody well stay kneeling.

And – you know what – why not scrub the floor while you're about it?

Believe me, I don't hold a candle for so-called Doctor Harold Shipman.

Doctor? Doctor???

Pull the other!

Serial killer, more like. And all-round nasty piece of work.

Ask yourself this. What sort of a doctor cold-bloodedly murders his patients?

Not any sort of doctor I know.

Doctors are meant to heal people. Not make them worse.

And one thing's for sure.

Once you're dead, no amount of pills will make you better.

In the old days, doctors made you well again. They didn't go around killing you.

Or not unless they had to, for medical reasons.

But these days, the whole medical profession's up the spout.

What kind of world are we living in?

You get a bit of a sniffle, call the doctor. And the next thing you know he's pulled up your sleeve and he's administering a fatal injection to you.

And what about his missus, Primrose Shipman?

Blimey. There's a woman who's let herself go.

Like so many modern women – Ginger Spice is another – she should make more of an effort. Take a bit of exercise. Cut down on the carbohydrates.

Then – and only then – can she start looking for another bloke.

Okay, she's no good around the house. The Shipman home was in a terrible state. If you gave her a scrubbing brush, she'd probably eat it with ketchup.

But some blokes prefer the slatternly type. The type who sit on their fat arses all day, leaving all their muck exactly as they found it.

Brave farmer Tony Martin, for one.

What's more, the bloke's a bachelor.

After all this time, he must be gagging for it.

Are you thinking what I'm thinking, Primrose?

Go for it, love. You might never get a better chance.

Clive James

My time is set well fair to say farewell to TV. After twenty years of quality programme making, I have decided that saying "goodbye" is not only a "good buy", but the very best "bye-bye" money can buy. So "by Clive James" will now become "'bye, Clive James". If I have an itch, it is for a switch, and that switch is marked "off". Tears will be shed, but, as Goethe once said, no man can cry without shedding tears.

As personalities go, I was always much more a "person" than an "ality". While others were self-promoting, the only self I promoted was the pro who said, "moting doing". In my self-deprecation, it was myself that I deprecated. It was not long before I was universally admired for my modesty. It was generally agreed, even by me, that I was a whole lot more interesting than the characters I interviewed. While lesser characters said, "Look at me," I would take the phrase, turn it on its head and spin it into stimulating paradox. "Me at look" I would shout, and the world would catch its breath.

If ten years is a long time, twenty years is a whole lot longer. Talking on television, it is on television that I have talked. My talk has been designed for others to hear – and hearing what I have to say has truly set them talking. Some have called television a Magic Lantern, and it is for its magic that this particular lantern will be remembered.

It is only by keeping myself in the foreground that I have been able to keep my subjects in the background. Looking back at some of my classic self-deprecating documentaries – *Clive James Meets Denise Van Outen in a Massage Parlour, Clive James's Postcard from Stringfellow's, Clive James Meets Baby Spice in his Swimming Trunks,* and the mould-breaking *Clive James Meets Clive James and Likes What He Sees* – I have learnt to marvel at my ability – at once able and marvellous – to subsume myself intellectually in my subject.

In my famous *Postcard from Russia,* I memorably spoke to the hard-working Russian writer Alexander Solzhenitsyn. The interview took place in Siberia, in a makeshift sauna populated by dusky young Russian ladies whose birthday suits fitted them like gloves – gloves I wanted to place on my own hands, though I turned out to be all fingers and thumbs. And as I went all *gooey* in their *laps,* I asked Alexander about his own time in the *gooey-lag.* Was it ever this pleasant, I wondered?

Rarely have the skills employed by the interviewer been by the interviewer so skillfully employed. When Solzhenitsyn answered, I spoke carefully; listening hard, I hardly listened:

CJ *(voice over)*: Alexander Solzhenitsyn is a towering writer with a long beard whose stories are as tall as his memory is broad and his fingers are short. His writer's eyes – two, one on each side of his nose, both open at the same time, each viewing the world from their unique perspective – watch carefully, as if to say, "Is this really the famously self-deprecating Clive James?"

When the authorities told him to "Stay! Stay!" he said no, no, he wanted to archipela-go-go. So the first question I asked was as blunt as a sickle – and twice as sharp:

CJ: Alexander, when I was a young boy growing up in Australia, I'd sometimes drink a pint of Brown Wallaby Home Brew and then plant a sicky on my mum's begonia – and, let me tell you, she would persecute me for it! You, too, have faced persecution in your own country, Alexander – I guess they must have something against beards, eh?! – and you were denied access to a lot of Literature. You may even have missed my own classic *I Wanged My Donger Up a Kookaburra*. So what I wanted to know, Alexander, is this: through all those years of persecution, you remained loyal to an ideal – but, tell me, was that ideal Posh – or was it Ginger?

Alexander Solzhenitsyn: I – er – I – don't –

CJ: You're not going to tell me it was Baby! No? Scary? Blimey! Did I tell you, I once dated Naomi Campbell? Talk about intelligent! Her mind was as curvaceous as her breasts and her breasts were every bit as bouncy as her mind. Well, thanks for talking to us, Alexander, good luck with the old book – and now we "mos-go" to "Moscow" – where the spirit of Boris Pasternak haunts a rather special lap-dancing club...

––––––––––

The past is long, and top-quality TV is long-past. It may have looked simple, but its simplicity was highly complex, and it was a complex that was by no means inferior. Inferior decoration is not the same as interior decoration. The two words have many letters in common, but they mean something quite different. My programmes may have been interior, but they were never inferior.

But sadly, the days are over when one could talk to Norman Mailer about Henry Miller on BBC television while being massaged by a young lady with bazonkers the size of War and Peace, Leo Tolstoy's magisterial masterpiece, which I myself have read in the original Russian nearly all the way through. The cult of celebrity has changed all that.

In dumbing down our culture, it is our culture that has been dumbed down. It was Proust who Searched for Lost Time, but he might have been Searching for Lost Radio Times too. A once-proud magazine is now a magazine that was proud, once. I doubt that television landmarks such as "Clive James and Denise Van Outen Say Let's Party in New Year '98 with Torvill and Dean" would ever get made these days. In the old days, one would study Oriental Languages to degree standard as a preparation for examining the sociological and cultural effect on naked Japanese men of swallowing live spiders while sitting in gunge. But in these pap-filled days, they're letting anyone do it, education be damned.

Cultural television has been shown the back door, and that door is marked "Back Door". The jewel is in the crown no more. The crown has drowned, causing the free world to frown. Around town, the crown is a clown, and its colour is brown, proving that rust is no substitute for trust. But as the delighful (and, incidentally, highly intelligent) Britney Spears told me in my seminal *Clive Meets Britney Down Under*, a bust is a must for intellectual thrust.

Cecil Beaton's Unexpurgated Christmas

Dec 25th 1970: Chez Moi. Perfectly ghastly church service au matin. Vicar plump, ill-shaven and brutish, ditto choirboys, clad in simply hideous turquoise and shrimp vestments, utterly unwaisted, did less than nothing for their podgy little piggy figures, great fat bottoms swaying this way and that.

We are forced to drone our way through "Away In A Manger". What sort of bedroom is that? Those 1st Century Jews were so stubbornly lazy and drab when it came to making any effort at home decoration. And if there was no room at the Inn, they should jolly well have got their secretary to book them one in advance. Given the choice, I would frankly rather be Away in a Mansion: infinitely more accommodating, and so much more glamorous. Even Away in a Manager might be preferable, though one would have to do something about those awful "lapel badges" they insist upon wearing on their cheap, ill-cut, two-piece suitings.

Three Kings, albeit from the East, would be a godsend at that time of year, I suppose, but what on earth were they thinking about when they went on to admit all those rank, soggy, common little shepherds, with ghastly soiled sheets for headgear, and nothing but "open-toed" sandals – sandals! – for footwear?

Babies are quite bad enough, but no one should countenance sheep, let alone oxen, in the home. One must, of course, remain ever-grateful that one was not invited for that first Christmas – in Bethlehem, of all places! So suburban! Yet with a few elegant swags and drapes, some simple yet sympathetic lighting and a hairdresser with just a touch of style, one could have improved their image no end. No more the dowdy "Virgin" hiding behind that ugly blue headscarf and shapeless "robe": I would have dressed her in the most marvellous cobalt silk ballgown, displaying the merest hint of cleavage, perhaps with extravagant bell-sleeves, her hair teased and swept back.

Would she have needed a handbag? In her position, she might, I suppose, have been able to get away without one, but I personally would have gone for something petite but gracious, yet – a diamond here, an emerald there – positively dripping with understated wealth.

As for Joseph – nothing to say for himself, terrible dried-up old brute, bearded and grubby, mottled wind-swept cheeks, fingernails bitten to the core, all the while casting those furtive, chip-on-shoulder, dark looks this way and that, unwanted hanger-on par excellence – I would have sent him packing.

The Queen Mother invites one over for a Christmas drink.

"You have never looked so positively radiant, ma'am! I don't know how you do it!" I exclaim as she greets us. In fact, she looks like an overweight hippopotamus – and an ill-bred hippopotamus at that – and I know perfectly well how she does it: by pigging out on chocolate bon-bons and knocking back cheap house champagne from dawn 'til dusk. She may indeed look radiant, but then so too did Hiroshima.

"Cecil, will you sit next to The Queen?" she says. I had high expectations, but once again I was dreadfully let down. Alas, The Queen is no beauty. Far from it. A card-carrying midget, of course – she surrounds herself with corgies to lend her height – and she is not improved by that hair, which is got up to look like Mrs Mopp. It does rather rankle that she makes so little effort when one "drops round". She obviously sees herself as fearfully "important" – all superior smiles and hoity-toity gestures – yet she has zero sex appeal, and would be better suited to serving behind the haberdashery counter at Maison Woolworth. Her embonpoint, too, is crudely obtrusive and tiresomely invasive, so that for one's personal safety one is forced to duck every time she turns round.

"What a marvellous complexion Her Majesty has!" I purr sympathetically to Louis Mountbatten (raddled old mascara'ed buggeriste got up like a pantomime admiral, all over-shone epaulettes and hideous buttons) upon adjourning to the withdrawing room. "And such natural grace and dignity!" Manners are so desperately important in this coarse and vulgar age.

––––––––––––

Giving presents for Christmas is, of course, unforgiveably common.

Receiving them, on the other hand, is a sign of good breeding.

I have stored the many presents I have received beneath my Christmas tree – a simple yet stylish Dutch elm – and I "open" them with a pure silver paperknife, immediately disposing of their gaudy wrappings with my private flame-thrower.

Darling Diana Cooper has given me a gold wristwatch. Bless

her. Tilted at a certain angle, I can see my face in it. I will not breathe a word against Diana. This is just one of the reasons I keep a diary, in which one can write words rather than breathe them. Diana was always the most sparkling conversationalist and divine beauty. That is why I am so very full of sympathy for her now that she has turned into a wrinkled old sow and a Grade 1 bore, incapable of giving even her closest friends anything more original than gold wristwatches for Christmas. How my heart goes out to her!

An Yves St Laurent floppy bow-tie from my dear old friend Wallis, The Duchess of Windsor. I dote on her. She was never what one might describe as a "beauty", of course, but she had a certain something, namely the then Prince of Wales. She was witty, in a caustic, boot-faced, daggers-drawn sort of way, but her looks now make her rather more suited to the Ghost Train at Chessington Zoo, I fear, than to a Royal Palace.

Tring! At the unearthly hour of 8.30 pm, the doorbell goes. "Good King Wenceslas looked out, on the feast of Stephen!" sing a motley group of embittered carol singers, their cheeks pinched and scarlet in the freezing cold.

"I care not a fig whether Mr Wenceslas looked out or not!" I exclaim, slamming the door firmly on their grotesque faces. "He may have styled himself Royal, but he came from what is now Czechoslovakia, and is of no consequence whatsoever! Be off with you!"

Oh, the sheer crude ghastliness of Christmas! As a great friend of Lord Jesus, I know he would be absolutely horrified at what he has now set in motion.

Janet Street-Porter: My Life

Tough shit.

That's basically what I thought when I came out of my mother's womb to hear her screaming her bloody head off.

Why wouldn't the old cow shut the fuck up, that's what I wanted to know.

I'd only been alive a few minutes, and everyone wanted to see me, not her. And there she was, making the most godawful scene. She obviously couldn't bear the thought that I had arrived on the scene to upstage her. So I resolved there and then to clear the fuck out of her life the first moment I possibly could.

Being born was great. But the initial excitement soon wore off.

All the time I was a baby my mother did her level best to make me feel inferior by dressing me in baby clothes rather than the red and yellow striped PVC trousers and bright orange skintight sleeveless polo neck I'd have looked so much better in. Honestly, talk about what a bloody cow.

And whenever I wanted to go anywhere she'd just stick me in a pram to increase my sense of humiliation and make me feel small. Why couldn't she understand that I was better than that, that one day I would see it as like totally normal basically to be riding in a stretch limo with my friends top superstar Elton John and the lovely David Furnish and talking besottedly about cutting-edge conceptual art and the very latest in modern music.

My parents and I had nothing in common, no conversation, no small talk, nothing. Just imagine my horror when aged five I found they'd booked me into a primary school. How bloody dare they. "Don't you know who I am?" I said, but they wouldn't bloody listen, would they, no way.

The Perivale Primary School was something rotten. The uniform was a total turn-off, the teachers had no like sense of style whatsoever and the service was truly appalling. In the school breaks they'd expect us to drink this unpleasantly lukewarm free school milk. Ugh! Why would I bother with drinking that muck when in just a few years time I could expect to be drinking a full range of exotic rum-based cocktails with my good friends The Pet Shop Boys at Park Lane's famous Metropolitan Bar.

Our family holidays were rotten too. Who wants to end up in a caravan in some crappy resort, specially when it's fucking raining outside. Not me and that's for sure.

I tried to inject some fun into the proceedings by letting go of the brake and pushing our cheap and nasty family Vauxhall over the cliff but that turned out to be just one more thing they didn't approve of, didn't it?

Talk about whingeing. "If you push another car over the cliff, my girl, I'll teach you a lesson you'll never forget!" ranted my father, in natural bullying mode, "And you can put that knife down while you're about it, young lady."

———————————

My father never failed to make me feel inferior. Once I was putting on my false eyelashes and my fluorescent mini to go out for a night on the town and he stopped me at the door saying, "And where, may I ask, do you think you're going to dressed like that, young lady?"

I informed him that I was go down The Easy Beat club in Berwick Street to hang out with the groovy crowd. "But you're not yet seven years old," he said, blocking my way in his cheap drab dowdy grey suit.

"Shut the bloody fuck up!" I responded. He was such a bloody misery, always whingeing about something or other. All in all, I guess I was just too sophisticated for him and my equally dreary mother.

———————————

But soon I was dyeing my hair with the new wonder lightener Poly Blond and scoring drinks with fanciable blokes down the Tottenham Court Road.

This was the dawn of the Sixties and it was lined up to be so totally a happening decade. For starters, there was super-trendy alternative music with Tommy Steele and Frank Ifield. I once met Frank Ifield down the Roxy and might have given him a shag but got bored after a few minutes and decided to settle for a hand-job.

Then there was cutting-edge comedy with Arthur Askey and Cyril Fletcher. I didn't half fancy a shag with little Arthur Askey, but even though I was totally besotted once he'd told me yet another of his tedious jokes I got bored shitless and dumped him. And the Black and White Minstrels weren't much better at shagging either, but that's another story. Would I like to fly in their beautiful, their beautiful ballooooooon? No I bloody wouldn't, guys, so why not fuck off.

On the radio one day halfway through Two-Way Family Favourites, I heard that President Kennedy had been shot in Detroit. Typical! He'd just gone and interrupted my favourite record. I had just been thinking of going to America, and now he goes and gets himself assassinated. Men! I mean, talk about upstaging.

Anyway, the assassination was quite interesting at the beginning but the initial excitement soon wore off.

Carnaby Street in the Sixties was the only place to be. It totally swang, and I was like right in the centre of it. I once met top Italian film director Antonio Knee who was working on his totally happening film Blow Job. He wanted a shag, only he was too fat for my taste, but I gave him one anyway, behind what used to be Pontings Department Store just off Kensington High Street.

One day I got married to a man called whatever but by the evening the initial excitement had worn off. There was nothing on television that night – these were the days before I had totally stamped the medium with my iconoclastic and innovatory approach – so I met up with a Dutchman but after a bit of squidging about on the mattress he turned out to be quite boring too.

I wanted new music, new art, new things, new experiences. I wanted to do everything once before the initial excitement wore off – and I was determined not to remain stuck in dreary old Perivale a second longer. So when my mother tried once again to make me feel small by asking me what I wanted to do that day I replied, "I can't stand being with you one fucking minute longer, you miserable old cow, don't you know who I bloody am?" and walked out forever.

It was a bold move the ordinary people of this country applauded. Twenty years later, when I was appointed executive producer of the mouldbreaking "Up Your Arse Total Grooverama" show on BBC2, it ran for three series.

And the rest is history.

Diana at 40: What if She Had Lived?

Top medium RITA ROGERS first met Diana in 1994. The two quickly became friends.

When she last visited me, just a week before her tragic and untimely death, I told Princess Diana that she was soon to meet the man of her dreams, and that they would settle down and bring up four beautiful children together, before setting up a top-of-the-range bed-and-breakfast with full tea and coffee-making facilities in a gorgeous location just down the road from me in Chesterfield. He would have been a Scorpio with Neptune rising, either a successful ironmonger or something to do with computers, first name either Steve or Dave, hobbies football, gardening and greyhounds, favourite food steak, favourite colour blue. But tragically it was not to be. My only regret is that I didn't warn her, due to unforeseen circumstances.

Royal biographer ANTHONY HOLDEN, 59, first met Diana in 1992. The two quickly became friends.

Her 40s would, I believe, have been the making of Diana. Anyone who, like me, knew and cared for her can only hope she would by now have found the right man to marry second time round. He would not, before you ask, have been Dodi. Dodi was not, before you ask, her type at all. She preferred a somewhat older man, perhaps a divorcee, possibly an award-winning journalist and biographer who was not afraid to stand up to Buckingham Palace – and a committed republican to boot.

Together I feel sure that the two of them would have been taken to the public's heart as they flew around the globe spreading goodwill, while he continued to write, but her wealth allowed him to pursue his more serious work, free from the need to churn out half-baked nonsense for the newspapers.

Needless to say, the Prince of Wales would have been sick with jealousy towards Diana's beloved new spouse, and filled with remorse that he had not made the effort to get to know him better. But I hope and pray, that, after a few years had passed, he would have had the grace to acknowledge that the best man won, and to put all those years of envy and bitterness behind him.

Leading film director MICHAEL WINNER first met Diana in 1991. The two quickly became friends.

Shortly before her dramatic death, Princess Di privately agreed to take a leading role in my forthcoming Death Wish 4 – and very good she would have been too. The lady had star quality. Aged 40, she would have enjoyed the international stature of a new Diana Dors. If my good friend Charlie Bronson were still alive, they'd have made a super couple – and I'd have been absolutely delighted to be Best Man at the nuptials. You know, there's no more unpleasant sight than a dead policeman. What a superb Patron of my Dead Coppers' Trust Diana would have been – and she sported a fabulous figure for the gentlemen too!

LYNDA LEE POTTER, 63, first met Diana in 1993. The two quickly became friends.

On her 40th birthday, Diana would be taking a long, hard look at herself in a full-length mirror. An extra cream bun here, a stolen chocolate biscuit there – she would have been piling on the pounds like nobody's business.

10 stone. 12 stone. 14 stone. 16 stone. By now, strangers in the street would be mistaking her for Ann Widdecombe. Brutally ejected by the cold, heartless Windsors from her £2m apartment in Kensington Palace, she would have moved into a dingy bed-sit on the outer fringes of Earls Court, a rapidly-diminishing pile of 50 pence pieces beside her rusty gas meter.

Every morning as she scurried past the front door of her old flat in Colherne Court on her way to the Job Centre, she would wonder to herself where it all went wrong. Once, she could have had her pick of luxury frocks from some of Britain's top designers. But now it was Dorothy Perkins or nothing.

Suddenly, a Jaguar sweeps past, filled with leading figures from the glamorous world of music, restaurants and haute couture who used to woo Diana with fancy gifts and top-of-the-range holidays abroad.

But now they don't give tragic, overweight, single mum scrounger Diana a second glance.

It's hard not to feel desperately sorry for her.

But – and I say this as a valued admirer – *she brought it on herself.*

Gerald Kaufman's
Summer Holiday

Monday: I am persuaded by an albeit rare outbreak of sun to honour the beach with a visit. But I first proceed to a shop, the proprietor of which maintains a meagre display of sun-hats. "Pray, sir, are you in possession of any headwear relevant to my needs, albeit of a type that does not bear either this or a slogan similar?" I ask, pointing to a hat bearing the elitist legend, "Kiss Me Quick".

"Sorry, mate," he replies.

"Please neither interrupt nor hector me, my dear sir," I riposte, in my usual measured tones. "If I have no wish to be kissed, quickly or otherwise, neither can I be persuaded to be heckled. Please assist informed democratic debate by answering my simple question – yes or no?"

"No."

"Yes or no?"

"No."

"Ah! Did you say yes?"

"No. I said no."

Touché! Through a combination of fastidious cross-examination and razor-sharp instinct, I have cornered the aforesaid gentleman into admitting that he has no appropriate sun-hats for the purchase thereof.

"In the circumstances, I am not prepared to continue our discussion," I say, turning on my heels in a manner reminiscent of Gene Kelly in his evergreen if over-rated "Singin' In The Rain". The gentleman is flabberghasted, little realising he has just taken on an opponent who, as the linchpin of every major post-war Labour Government, has established himself as something of an expert at the art of debate.

———————

Tuesday: Having traced a sun-hat, I venture down to the seashore. I am frankly appalled by the conditions that greet me. I make haste to summon a duty officer.

"This standard of flooring is wholly, but wholly, unacceptable," I complain.

"But it's sand," he whines. "People expect it on a beach."

"That is not the issue," I remonstrate. "The issue is whether they have a right to expect something of an altogether higher standard. You'll hear more of this."

"But the kiddies like to build castles with it," he whined.

"If you wish me to point a Building Standards Officer in your direction, so be it," I rejoin. "But I would have you know you are talking to someone who served upon the Royal Commission into the Construction Industry, 1969-73, so I am something of an expert in the field. And what, may I ask, is all that water doing there?"

"It's the sea!" he said.

"Please don't it's-the-sea me – this is a very serious matter," I correct him. "And it may well lead to a number of alarming consequences. That 'sea' could make a number of elderly or underprivileged persons intolerably damp. The issue at stake is the public's right to wear dry clothes, free from the fear of drowning. If it is cleared away by tomorrow at the latest, I will say no more about it."

Wednesday: In a scene reminiscent of Bette Davies in her classic "Now, Voyager," I proceed gracefully along the pier. In my morning perambulations, I like to devote between five and seven minutes to recalling a selection of words of wit and wisdom it has been my great good fortune to coin over the years. In 1979, Margaret Thatcher became, I regret to say, one of the unlucky recipients of one of my classic put-downs. "Will the Rt Hon Lady kindly tell the House," I said, "why one so fastidious in her personal appearance seems so keen to make such a thorough mess of the country unfortunate enough to have her as Prime Minister?!!!!!" Her career never quite recovered, and just ten short years later she was out of a job. Then in 1983, I described Willie Whitelaw as "a very large man in an equally large suit". Need I add that it brought the House down?!

Halfway through this trip down memory lane, I am interrupted by a coarse brigand. " 'Ere, clear off my private property, you frog-faced slap-headed git!" he shouts. I have never been so insulted in my life. I inform him of my firm intention to report his ill manners to the duty officer at the local police station.

Thursday: I pay a visit to a Magic Show in the theatre at the end of the pier. This is not, I should add, my usual fayre. As one who has recently taken in both Sophocles' Electra at the Donmar Warehouse and Wagner's Ring Cycle at the Coliseum, not to mention a delightful trip to Stratford as the personal guest of the artistic director, I have no need to boast of my commitment to high culture.

The conjuror, who seems a very pleasant individual, asks me to pick a card, any card, not to tell anyone what it is, and to place it back in the pack. This act I duly perform. He then makes an extravagant albeit ostentacious display of shuffling before throwing all the cards in the air and stabbing a single card with a dagger. "And what was the name of your card, sir?" he says, as a drum rolls.

"I am not prepared at this juncture to reveal that information," I reply.

"*Please* tell me the name of your card, sir," he asks.

"You are referring to information I solemnly agreed hitherto should remain confidential," I reply.

The act peters out without, so far as one can see, any recognisable "magic" forthcoming.

"You didn't want to do it like that," I tell the conjuror as he slouches off. Of course, I am something of an expert in the field of family entertainment, having personally founded the British Satire Movement in the early 1960s.

Friday: Pursuant to Esther Williams' eminently cherishable albeit flawed performance in the classic Bathing Beauty (1944), I decide to dip my little toe in the sea. Like much modern opera – of which, I freely admit, I am something of an expert – I find it not altogether to my taste. Staring aghast at all the other bodies on the beach, I cannot turn a blind eye to their aura of social exclusivity and unabashed elitism, with their air of "getting on well", "sun-bathing" and their conspicuous consumption of highly expensive "ice-creams". Memo to Tony from something of an expert in these matters: It is time to abolish the beach as an elitist meeting-place of sunworshippers and seabathers. Thus expunged, it will become a much more civilised environment for those who are able better to appreciate it, such as my own good self.

The Brit Awards

ZOE BALL: Wooh!

FRANK SKINNER: Hey, love the way you say "Wooh". Fantastic!

ZOE BALL: Wooh!

FRANK SKINNER: There she goes again! Wooh! It's contagious! That means it's sort of catching!

ZOE BALL: Wooh!

FRANK SKINNER: Tell you what, Zoe. That Jordan, eh? Talk about Big Bazookas!

ZOE BALL: Wooh!

FRANK SKINNER: Last time I saw Bazookas that big was on... well, on Jordan actually!!!

ZOE BALL: Wooh!

FRANK SKINNER: Now we've got something so special for you it's more special than you can possibly imagine, it's that special. Ladies and Gentlemen, please give it up for... KYLIE!!!!

KYLIE: *Lalalalalalala*
lalalalalalala
lalalalalalala
Yajis cairn gitchew adderma yed
Yajis cairn gitchew adderma yed
Yajis cairn gitchew adderma yed
lalalalalalala
lalalalalalala
lalalalalalala

ZOE BALL: WOOH!

FRANK SKINNER: Classic! Classic! Didja see that pert bum on Kylie, didja? Classic!

ZOE BALL: Wooh!

FRANK SKINNER: Now to introduce the nominations for Consignia/Nuclear Fuels Best International Top-Selling Artist with a Name Ending in Y, we have a woman who I'll always think of for giving of her BREAST – whoops! silly me! I meant to say giving of her BEST – honest!! – yes, a warm nipple – I mean RIPPLE! – of applause for DARRYL HANNAH!

ZOE BALL: Wooh!

FRANK SKINNER: Mmmm. You're looking lovely, Darryl.

DARRYL HANNAH: Hi.

FRANK SKINNER: As I say, you're looking lovely. Really lovely.

ZOE BALL: Wooh!

FRANK SKINNER: Fabulous. Right. Yes. Well. Really lovely. Erm.

ZOE BALL: Wooh!

FRANK SKINNER: Really great. So, perhaps you should tell us who won. Erm.

DARRYL HANNAH: And the nominations for the Sainsbury Supersaver Best International Top-Selling Spicy Condiments Artist with a Name Ending with Y are: Shaggy, Baggy, Haggy, Draggy, and Saggy. And the winner is... yes... SHAGGY!

ZOE: Wooh!

SHAGGY: *Gotta finda solu-sharn*
To whirl revolu-sharn
And get a comfy cush-sharn
And sit on it to avoid confu-sharn!

SHAGGY: Wow! First of all I want to thank everybody who made it all possible that's Brian and Ray and Miles my personal trainer and Jim and Geoff in the office and Reg my driver and Graham and Dana in charge of the jewellery and Julie and then there's Ray in Accounts and Stuart my lawyer and Terry who's in charge of my Property Portfolio and Mike my Stockbroker and not forgetting everybody in Personnel specially Sue and Geoff, or did I just say Geoff, and my Mum and Dad and sister June and Dave and all the helicopter crew, and and Pam and Nigel and the rest of my household, outdoor and leisure centre staff and the whole HOT SHOT REVOLU-SHARN MASSIVE!!!

ZOE BALL: Wooh!

FRANK SKINNER: Yes. Right. Um. Yes. Now to introduce the nominations for HSBC Gold MasterCard Best International World Banking Act, please give it up for the mean and moody Mr Russell CROWE!

RUSSELL CROWE: Whatdyou feckin mean by that you feckin little fecker, tek it ep yeh feckin airse, mite.

ZOE BALL: Wooh!

FRANK SKINNER: Great! It's a great joy to meet you, Russ! Yes! So let's have the winner. Erm.

RUSSELL CROWE: And the winner is... So Sullied Crew!

SO SOLID CREW: *Yo yo yo yo die no no no no cry*
wo wo wo wo why bo bo bo bo hi
lo lo lo lo lo sky so so so so bye!

ZOE BALL: WOOH!

FRANK SKINNER: Not too long 'til the end now. Fabulous! Should be off in under the hour! Great! Did you see the boobs on those dancers, didja? Talk about globe artichokes, eh? Eh?

ZOE BALL: Wooh!

FRANK SKINNER: Great knockers! And I'm not talkin' 'bout the type you get on doors sometimes instead of an electric bell in kind of old-fashioned houses! Anyway. Right. Um. Yes. To introduce the man who has achieved the Montsanto Lifetime Achievement Award for Outstanding Achievement in Achieving Outstanding Achievement, please re-re-re-welcome – KYLIE!!!

KYLIE: *Lalalalalalalalalalala*
Yajis cairn gitchew adderma yed
Yajis cairn gitchew adderma yed

KYLIE: This is a guy who has sold more than 100 million records at over £15 each from all the people around the world, regardless of race, colour and creed, grossing a remarkable £1500 million worldwide for his record company – Ladies and Gentlemen, give it up for... STING!

STING: I just wanna say one thing to all you struggling no-hopers out there – always remember that MUSIC IS ITS OWN REWARD!

STING: *Freefree, setme free*
Freefree, setme free
Freefree, setme free
Freefree, setme free

ZOE BALL: WOOH! Wooh!

FRANK SKINNER: Can I go home now?

Iain Duncan Smith
June 2003

MONDAY

Onward and upward. That's my motto. Defeat? That's a four-letter word. And not one that crops up in my vocabulary.

If you are a General leading his troops into the trenches, you're not going to be deflected from victory just because a bombshell happens to have fallen on your head. Far from it. Okay, so your head has been sliced off. But you've still got two perfectly good legs. And let me add this. The British people have never set much store by heads. That is their inalienable right. And I don't intend to see it squandered.

This afternoon, I put through a call to Michael Howard. I bear him no rancour. Not a bit of it. I wish to offer him the benefit of my years in high office. And I hope to make it clear that I am available to put my experience at his service.

Michael is out. Busy man! Poor chap – I bet he now wishes he had a bit of my time for leisure activities! Of course he does.

At last, I can get on with the things that really matter. After all, I have my hobbies – what Denis Healey once called a winterland. This morning, I resume work on a long-standing project that has been sorely neglected these past two years. As every dedicated aero-modeller will be aware, the dog-fight double – the Messerschmitt and Spitfire, accurately constructed and painstakingly painted in the correct Humbrol paint colours – is an ambitious project for anyone to take on.

But it is a project I intend to see through.

TUESDAY

By lunchtime, I have finished laying the instructions out and have begun the onerous task of placing all the constituent parts – and there are well over 50 of them! – in the correct order for easy assembly. Once I get up a head of steam, I estimate this project will have been completed by the end of the week. Then, and only then, will I embark on the most almighty dog-fight! May the best man win! Though personally I'd back the British Spitfire against the Jerry Messerschmitt anytime! (Or is that what they call "politically correct"!!??!!) Onward and upward!

Michael H. has still not called back. I put another call through to his office, informing them I have mislaid his home number and could they let me have it? They tell me they can pass on any message. Before I call off, they ask me to remind them whether I spell my surname with a hyphen or without.

WEDNESDAY

Actually, solitaire is a very good game. Around mid-morning, the fuselage of the Messerschmitt began to get a bit fiddly, and I'd snapped one of the propellors in frustration, so I thought I'd take a breather. Betsy was having her hair done, and Michael still hadn't rung back (frankly he should get his staff in shape – if they can't pass on a simple message then how the bloody heck are they going to win an election?!!!) so I looked around for something to do. And there was the solitaire! The first game, I was left with eleven balls, the second game with thirteen, the third – owing to a technical setback – with seventeen. It's a record of consolidation and growth of which I am justly proud. My mission is to get down to one by Christmas. And I intend to do it my way. So much for the chattering classes! I'm happy to place my faith in the British people!

Just as I am embarking on a fourth game, my loyal old colleague Michael Ancram phones to see how I'm coping with what he calls my "new-found freedom". Good of him to call. Pick yourself a halfway decent ADC and he'll never let you down. I tell him of the strides I'm making with the Dog-fight Double. He tells me that Central Office have been on at him about the return of my key, and how he looks forward to having a longer chat before too long.

THURSDAY

Typical instruction manual! They make it absolutely impossible to fit wings on each side of the Spitfire. So, after giving the matter much thought, I've settled, ingeniously, for fitting both wings to the same side, and doing the same for the Messerschmitt, so the impending dog-fight will be fair.

I'm just playing around with the glue when Betsy puts her head around the door with a sympathetic smile and says that the first reviews of my novel have just come in. "Great! Onward and upward!" I say, "Let's see 'em!"

She says it'll save a lot of bother if she just reads out the best bits.

I'm all ears, but she's taking her time.

"Come on!" I say.

"I'm still looking," she says. Then at last she reads one out. "This one says there's no one like Duncan Smith for mixing his metaphors and creating two-dimensional characters," she says.

"High praise," I say, scraping some glue off my forehead.

Onward and upward!

At long last, Michael Howard has rung back. Or at least a pleasant young lady his office. It's a courtesy call they're extending to all future Conservative backbenchers. They want the names and addresses of any wives and children, etc, so that Michael and Sandra can send us their seasonal greetings.

Before bed, I manage to squeeze a dozen games of solitaire into my hectic schedule. In the crucial game five, I have just nine balls left. A personal best – and one in the eye for the snobby metropolitan elite who despise the views and abilities of ordinary British people.

FRIDAY

This morning, I managed to keep a single Smartie going for three minutes forty-seven seconds! We're frankly talking Guinness Book of Records material here!

The rave reviews continue to flood in. At lunchtime, Betsy tells me that one critic has hailed it a triumph. Looking over her shoulder, I see the exact phrase is "a triumph of self-delusion". But the point holds.

A Christmas card from Michael and Sandra, complete with every good wish for the coming year. One for the mantelpiece!

As predicted, the Messerschmitt lost the dog-fight to the plucky Spitfire, after finding itself covered in lighter fuel, taking a wrong turning and stupidly plunging into a lit match.

Tomorrow, I set to work on my new Airfix Hawker Hurricane.

Alain de Botton:
Padding Anxiety

CONTENTS
List of contents
Definitions
Thesis
Causes
How We Pad A Spare Page with a Graph
Solutions

III. Remind Me Again What the Problem Was

IV. A History of Padding

DEFINITIONS

Padding

  – soft material used to pad or stuff with

Pad

  – a piece of soft material used to reduce friction or jarring

  – a number of sheets of blank paper fastened together at one edge, for writing or drawing on

  – the fleshy underpart of an animal's foot

  – a guard for the leg and ankle in sports, part. cricket

  – *(colloq.)* a lodging, esp. a bedsitter or flat

  – lengthen or fill out a book with unnecessary, repetitive or irrelevant material

Ding

  – make a ringing sound

  – a bell-like noise

Ding-a-ling

  – the sound of a bell

Ding-dong

  – the sound of two chimes, as of two bells

  – an intense argument, perhaps resulting in a fight

Dinghy

  – a small inflatable rubber boat

THESIS

– That padding possesses an exceptional capacity to console authors, pacify publishers and detain readers.

– That padding, like all activities, has many uses: increasing the number of pages we hand in to our publishers; spurring us to write more and longer books; encouraging employment among those in print and paper-related industries; and filling out our bookshelves and those of our readers.

– That one of the most profitable ways of addressing the problem of padding lies in repeating what you have already said.

– That one of the most profitable ways of addressing the problem of padding lies in repeating what you have already said.

figure 1
an unpadded
page

figure 2
a padded
page

CAUSES

A Desire to Pad

It is according to how long we desire our completed book to be that we determine by how much – by what number or quantity of pages, words, letters and punctuations marks – to pad it out. Our gain in happiness will thus be commensurate with the accuracy with which we have calculated the sufficiency of padding.

A Devotion to Sub-Headings

The philosopher Michel de Montaigne formulated his thoughts in the 16th century, while either sitting down, standing up or – from time to time – going for a walk.

The Insertion of Celebrated Thinkers

This was three centuries before other philosophers, including John Ruskin, Friedrich Nietzsche, and Arthur Schopenhauer had their thoughts. But Montaigne would rarely go for a walk when it was dark outside, possibly for fear of bumping into a hazard, hurdle or obstruction.

A Lesson to be Learnt

From this we may learn that it is safest to think whatever thoughts we wish to think while remaining still, or at least to confine our motion to those moments when the available daylight is sufficient to enable us to see our way clearly ahead.

The Stating of the Obvious

To state the obvious, one is obliged to state the obvious. It is according to how frequently we state the obvious that we determine the frequency with which the obvious is stated.

Conclusion to Section on Causes

In the hands of the finest padders, padding becomes a worthwhile occupation. It takes a curmudgeonly spirit not to appreciate or recognise the beauty of the well-executed pad. Adam

Smith, Karl Marx and George Eliot have all contributed to the art of padding since the time of leading playwright William Shakespeare.

HOW WE CAN PAD A SPARE PAGE WITH A GRAPH

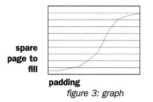

spare page to fill

padding

figure 3: graph

SOLUTIONS

I. Is There a Solution?

The basis of padding is to pose a question before then answering it. But first, we must pose the question: is there a solution?

II. There is a Solution

To the question "Is there a solution?" there is an answer, at once obvious, perfectly obvious and exceptionally obvious. To achieve it, we must endeavour to remove the question mark and transpose the first two words, before concluding "there is a solution".

III. Remind me again what the problem was

Socrates reminds us that, in our search for a solution, we must keep the problem uppermost in our minds.

IV. A History of Padding

i) Padding Under The Ancient Egyptians

To increase their efficiency at padding, the Ancient Egyptians would draw stickmen on ancient papyrus.

ii) Padding Under the Romans

Marcus Aurelius taught the Romans that padding leads to feelings of well-being.

iii) Padding in Medieval Times

There was a lot of padding in Medieval Times too. *The Canterbury Tales* by Geoffrey Chaucer demonstrate how *(continued on pages 94-326 plus index)*

Lady Thatcher

Fighting fit! Fighting fit! I may have the body of a weak and feeble woman, but I have the heart and stomach of a king! So let us to the battle, my friends! Kill! Kill! Kill!

If you'll just let me finish. We shall defend our island, whatever the cost, we shall fight on the beaches, we shall fight on the landing grounds, we shall fight in the fields and in the streets, we shall fight in the hills; we shall never surrender.

The lesson of my generation is that we should never give in. Never! Not ever! Never ever! Never! In those dark days of the war, when the Germans under Adolf Hitler and Gerhard Schroeder were busy attacking us, day in, day out, I turned to Winston in our secret bunker in Whitehall, looked him straight in the eye and said to him, "If you'll just let me finish, Winston – we must hold firm! This is no time for the wibble-wobble! We must fight to win!"

Well, all I can say is thank goodness Winston saw sense and heeded my warning. His greatest talent was always his extraordinary capacity to listen to advice.

The British are a stubborn, independent, freedom-loving people. My goodness, we are. If you'll just let me finish. That is the very essence of our character. We value our liberty like no other race on this earth. Look at the French, strutting about in their berets, with onions everywhere! But believe you me it was the good old British bowler hat that won the war. And we were never reliant on onions.

And that is why, once the war was won – not only by me, but by others too, for I've always been swift to give credit – we British said, loud and clear, "We shall not be bullied into submission. We shall have no truck with the forces of socialism and its iniquitous culture of dependency!" And that is why, in 1945, we followed our stubborn, fiercely independent instincts and voted Winston back in. And that is the lesson of history.

When I took over from Winston some good few years later, I was utterly determined to push on with his fierce and valiant struggle against the Europeans.

No wibble-wobble. No timid Timothys. No cowardly Cornelias. No surrender.

Our duty is to defend liberty and to show the world we have the determination so to do. I decided then and there that if we wished to save our beloved pound, there was only one course of action to take.

We would bomb Dresden.

And let me tell you this: IT WORKED! Our beloved pounds, shillings and pence were saved for future generations to enjoy and to pass onto their children, and their children's children. No more would the Nazi jackboot prevent us from paying for the Great British Banger with our shiny British tuppence-ha'penny.

But of course, Messrs Blair and Brown have learnt nothing from history. Nothing. Nil! Nit! In my day, if anything arose, you dealt with it quickly. You did not let it fester. That was not our way. But all is not lost. There is still time for Mr Blair to come to his senses. Today, I urge him to dip into history books, to take a deep breath – and to bomb Dresden once more!

And as our gallant young men – proud, decent Britons every one of them – prepare to carpet-bomb that wretched German city, let us remember for one moment why they are so doing.

It is so that the rest of us – we, the British race, who exported hope and freedom to the world – may pass on our earnings to future generations.

To my own children. To my own son, Mark. And my daughter. And their children, if any.

The family stands at the very heart of the British way of life. That for me is the message of Jesus Christ.

Jesus taught us that the British are a proud race, undaunted by tyrants, always ready to go it alone.

And the Christian faith teaches us, too, that higher taxation increases dependence on the state and by so doing diminishes personal liberty.

Forty days and forty long, dark nights. No – it cannot have been easy for Jesus in the desert as he fought off the demands and entreaties of our European masters. But I gave him the backbone. I said, "If you'll just let me finish. We shall never flinch from the struggle. A mighty burden rests upon our shoulders. The mighty burden of guarding our basic freedoms against the iniquity of a single currency. Let us be about our business!"

And, with the sheer grit and spunk of a true Briton, Jesus heeded well my advice: for the next two thousand years Britain remained independent of Europe and all its wiles. So if the Bible is to teach us anything, it is to trust to our doughty instincts and beware a single currency.

To luncheon with William and his equally unremarkable wife Ffion. What did I think of them? A *superb* couple, absolutely *superb*. Anyone who knows me knows that I would never call them *unremarkable*.

Unremarkable is not a word I use.

Sadly, Ffion struck me as unremarkable. Ffion! That's not the way I myself would have chosen to spell it.

"You should do something about that hair," I advised her, taking her to one side over a small glass of Scotch. "You don't want it like that! It's far too thin to wear that long! *You must get it cut*, my dear!"

After another small Scotch, I saw it as my duty to reach into my bag and pull out a decent pair of *strong British-made household scissors*, just right for the job in hand. Only last week, I used them to improve the Ancrams' curtains before setting sail on the unnecessary tassels on their cushions. "Stand still!" I told Ffion, "I'll see to it!" But the silly girl darted off to the other corner of the room. *Frit!* The girl was frit! So after another small Scotch I chased after her, scissors snapping in readiness.

"Anything the matter, Margaret?" It was William, standing in my way. "Out of the way, little fellow! I have a *job to do!*" I advised, drinking another small Scotch. Why *on earth* do one's junior ministers never let one finish the *job in hand?* Isn't it high time the little fellow realised that after twenty *very enjoyable years* as Prime Minister, I know what *needs to be done* with a pair of scissors?

If you'll just *let me finish!*

Frederic Raphael on Stanley Kubrick

The telephone rang. It had, I noted, a Kubrickian ring about it – all-powerful yet deferential, assured yet almost unassured. My instincts are rarely, if ever, faulty, wrong or fallacious. Sure enough it was Stanley Kubrick. He was a director I had been admired by for many years.

S.K. Is that the great Frederic Raphael?

F.R. C'est moi.

S.K. Gee whizz. Whaddayaknow! You speak French too! The guy's a genius!

It was indeed Stanley Kubrick. Though he had lived in England for many years, one could still detect in his speech the reliance on American colloquialism common to the intellectually insecure.

S.K. Zipadee-doo-dah! Well, hellzapoppin and Lordy-lordy! Have a nice day! Wanna write a movie for me, Freddie?

At this point, I was reminded of a similar experience when I won, or, as they used to say, was "elected" to a major scholarship in Classics at St John's College, Cambridge. I seem to remember using the telephone around that time, and this brought it all back: the constant plaudits for being the most intelligent student of my generation, the First Class Honours degree, the outstanding early achievements in the fields of screenwriting and fiction, the extraordinary career that found me ending up, quite against my expectations, widely regarded, not least by myself, as one of the greatest post-war writers of the 20th century. Extraordinary how evocative a simple telephone conversation can be.

I had known and admired Kubrick's work for many years. His "Paths of Glory" had particularly struck me: just two days before I saw it I had received this call from the great director Stanley Donen:

S.D. Freddie? Hi! Freddie, you're a genius! Whatever you write is pure gold-dust! Small wonder you're the most highly-regarded screenwriter in the whole US of A with over twenty superb screenplays to your credit! Ciao, Freddie!

And now I was to write for Kubrick himself. Pleased? He was thrilled. An entry in my journal records my first visit to Kubrick's home:

Journal entry 6.12.93. I am greeted at the door by Stanley. He is scruffy, and sports a beard, while I am smart, though never ostentatiously so, and clean-shaven. I permit myself a measure of intellectual levity in my replies to his somewhat coarse and brutish questions:

S.K. D'you wanna sandwich, Freddie?

F.R. A sandwich! Was it not Aristotle who said of the sandwich that it is little more than two slices of bread containing something other than bread? Or was it our very own F. Raphael? One so easily forgets!

S.K. Brown or white?

F.R. A question that, as Wedekind observed, most surely requires an answer. Have you read much Wedekind, Stanley? No? I thought not!

S.K. Brown or white?

As the above dialogue suggests, I have little fear that Kubrick is intellectually beyond my reach; I am not even sure how bright he is. He prefers to talk of sandwiches ("Brown or white?" he kept saying, as though it really mattered) than of literature and ideas. It is almost as though he is frightened by the very reach of my perception. Perhaps, deep down, he suspects I would be a greater director than he if only I could have been bothered. How I would love to reassure him, but my woeful integrity prevents me from uttering a dishonest word, dammit.

To employ a classical allusion, S.K. sometimes reminds me of a little animal or rodent – a grasshopper, maybe, or a goldfish – who feels himself overshadowed by a lion. It is the story of Herakles and the Minotaur all over again – with F.R. playing both roles, to S.K.'s piece of string. He greatly admires me, to be sure. But dost not the man who is full of admiration also feel daunted by the object of that admiration?

S.K. Freddie! Did I tell you you are a genius! Say, Freddie, how doya write realistic... dialogue that convinces... the reader that this is exactly what it was like to be... actually there? Think you can do it?

F. R. Sure, Stanley. You just need to... place dots here and there. And start some sentences with "and". And

124

S.K. have people interrupt each other and –

F.R. finish each other's sentences. Finally, if your main character's American, make sure you insert some obvious Americanisms, like –

S.K. Gee whizz, Freddie, too damn right! Hotdiggety-dawg! You betcha!

Mutatatis mutandi ergo sum. Stanley sought neither loyalty nor intimacy; both made betrayal more likely. In this, he is not unlike Marty Scorsese, Willie Wyler, Dirky Bogarde and Fayey Dunaway, all of whom have known and admired me from behind closed doors. But was there something deep inside in Stanley that held back from fuller intimacy? Something he once said suggested a certain reserve, a certain holding-off. I was making idle chit-chat when he came up with his telling remark.

F.R. *(sipping tea)* Stanley, are you, like moi, able to translate Aristotle into Spanish and back again via German? Oh, sorry – I was forgetting you never achieved a First at Cambridge!!!

S.K. Here's your money. Now piss off.

What did he mean? I guess I will never know. I never saw him again, but I rather suspect that, even in the grave, his admiration for me never wavers. *Amo, amas, amat, amsomarvellous, amanartist, amacunt...*

Stella McCartney

I was born on the 13th September like 1971. I was very small because I was just a baby. At that stage I wasn't like all that interested in fashion. My mum was probably my biggest influence. Mums are everyone's biggest influences, I s'pose. But my mum was my biggest influence basically because she was my biggest influence.

She was the kind of person who didn't give a toss, though in another way she really gave like a toss, probably more than anyone else I know. And that was like really, really weird.

What's it like growing up the daughter of Paul McCartney? Why do people always ask that? Is it just because I'm the daughter of Paul McCartney?

Like, in many ways it was kind of normal. I mean, like if

you're the kid of the local vicar, then you're, like, the kid of the local vicar, and people say, like, there goes the kid of the local vicar, or whatever, and you're going to be treated like the kid of the local vicar. And it was a bit like that for me, I suppose, only of course, my dad wasn't the local vicar, which might make it a bit different, in a way.

People are like always coming up and they're, like, how's your dad? So I'm like, yeah, how's YOUR dad? I mean, like, why are they always like coming up and saying, like how's your dad? Is it just because I'm the daughter of Paul McCartney? They don't know what it's like growing up the daughter of Paul McCartney. But, hey, I'm not knocking it. I just sometimes wish they'd ask me. But I'm glad they don't, because that would be like really, really weird.

Fashion is all about change. And not just change, but staying the same. Like, if I make a scarf, really stylish, really contemporary, really classic, it's sometimes difficult for people to get their heads round it. So I'm like, chill, you can't get your heads round a scarf. The scarf has to get its head round yours. Or not its head, because a scarf doesn't like have a head, it's not like human, but try getting your head around a scarf and you'll end up feeling like really, really weird. And that's why for me fashion is all about change. 'Cos, like, it's really, really weird but the only real way to change is to stay the same. Only different.

I had an idea for these gloves yesterday, and I was like, wow. I want to be really, really creative and like really push ideas to their furthest creation. My philosophy can be summed up as like, I want to take reality to the furthest reality, as part of the creative process. Because it's only by pulling ideas into their furthest creative reality that you can find where you're gonna like push them.

I wanted these to be very, very stylish, very, very classic and very, very contemporary. That was my whole philosophy of them, my whole glove philosophy. But first I had all these different like THINGS to work out, 'cos I have always paid very, very close attention to detail, 'cos basically I'm a very-close-attention-to-detail kind of person, that's just the way I am. So first – how many fingers on each glove? I thought about this and like really studied the whole human thing, and eventually I thought like – wow! – yup, it's got to be four fingers and a thumb. And not just four fingers and a thumb on one glove, but four fingers and a thumb on both gloves. And that's not because I've got anything against thumbs. I was always brought up to really appreciate thumbs, and I'm dead against people who are, like, against thumbs. No – it's because if you look at the average human hand and count, like I have, you'll find it's got four fingers and just one thumb, and that is what I wanted to, like, mirror, in my own gloves.

So I rang up my glovemaker and I'm like, a pair of gloves, four fingers and a thumb each, and I want it very, very stylish, very, very classic and very, very contemporary. And she transformed my vision into reality. And that was like really, really weird.

———————

Buttons. If you design a shirt, it'll need buttons. Most times. Unless it's a t-shirt. In which case it won't. Or not necessarily, anyway. That's my whole philosophy.

———————

So I'm like with my friends Naomi and Kate and Madonna and Gwyneth – to me they're just normal people, like me, like I don't go for that whole "celebrity" thing, they're just normal like people who happen to be Naomi and Kate and Madonna and Gwyneth, though I'm not saying they're not celebrities 'cos of course they are in fact like mega – and so I was with my friends Naomi and Kate and Madonna and Gwyneth and I was like, what shall we do now, and one of them, Kate, I think it was, was like, I know, let's watch some paint dry, that'd be like really, really weird.

So I get someone to paint like a wall or something, and we just sit there and watch the paint dry, and the whole experience is like very classic, very stylish, very contemporary. And Naomi's like, has the paint dried yet, and I'm like chill, because though the paint is paint in some ways it isn't paint, it's like just COLOUR on a sort of wall. And so we carry on watching it, and it's like rewarding because it's challenging, because it's challenging, and that's rewarding. And that's like really, really weird.

––––––––––––

What are my plans for the future? I don't think about the future but when I think about the future I'm like, the future's not here and now, and the future's not in the past, the future's like, in the future. And that's like really, really weird.

If I have a baby then I'll definitely be a working mum, but then again being a mum is a full-time job, so I'll have like two full-time jobs, so maybe I'll have to choose between being a mum and working, so the best like compromise is probably to be a working mum. But then again being a mum is a full time job. And that's like really, really weird.

––––––––––––

The thing about my clothes, like my basic whole creative vision concept, is I want them looking so they're like clothes you already might have but have forgotten about, or clothes you remember having somewhere but can't be bothered to like find, or clothes you would've thrown out if you'd thought of it but you haven't. They're exactly like normal people on the street are wearing – tops, trousers, skirts, dresses – but with a twist. And the like twist is we're talking £800, £900, £1000 for a pair of jeans, and the same for a top – and they don't like even match, which is great. And that's keeping costs really down, 'cos I'm not into the whole "celebrity designer really expensive hype" thing, I'm more interested in the kids on the streets, who could never afford my stuff anyway. And that's like really, really weird.

Max Hastings

After six years as a big hitter on the national stage, I'd learnt a thing or two about the competition. Over an expensive banquet at the Palace, I got the cut of the Queen Mother's gib pretty damned quick, for instance.

She was sitting next to me, short and buxom with far too much make-up. Not my type, but there we go. "So what d'you reckon the silver on this table is worth, ma'am?" I said, putting her at her ease, "500K? 600K? Bloody hell! That's nearly two years' salary!"

Let's not beat about the bush: The Queen Mother was a woman. Nothing wrong with that, of course. It remains my undiminished belief that the female of the species is more reliable, professional and idealistic than men, particularly when it comes to cooking and needlework. But something told me that it affected her judgement.

"Have you come far?" she asked me.

"Bloody daft question!" I replied with an engaging chuckle. With a deft stab borne of many years in waders, I speared my smoked trout starter and shoved it with a single thrust into my mouth, "Frankly, ma'am, I don't know why we pay you such a vast amount if you can't come up with something better to say than that!"

My jovial remark broke the ice superbly. From that point on, the old lady wisely shut her trap while I gave her the benefit of my experience. "With the greatest possible respect, ma'am," I began, in deference to her historic position, "your whole family would win first prize in the World-Class Nouveau Whingeing Stakes. What a bloody shower of second-rate bloody shits!"

My off-the-cuff comments helped clear the air. Just as importantly, they also gave the QM a first-rate view of what the nation was thinking. She responded magnificently, staring down at her plate, thinking seriously about what I had said.

"And pardon me, ma'am," I added, "but you really shouldn't toy with your food like that. It's common as muck. Either put up or shut up. If you can't manage any more, then place your knife and fork together and be done with it. No good blubbing. For god's sake, woman, don't act like something the cat's brought in!"

I then felt it judicious to clear the air. "What are you on these days?" I asked, sympathetically, "400K? 500K?"

Women divide into two categories. The kind who does what you tell her to. And the kind that doesn't. Frankly, I've got a hell of a lot of time for them both, in context. But one or two I can't abide.

I once had lunch with Mother Teresa at Wilton's. She was no bigger than the partridge on my plate. In fact, I was half-tempted to pour my remaining gravy over her. I could have downed her in a couple of mouthfuls and still had room for a decent rice pudding.

"God helps those who help themselves," I advised her. "You're frankly barking up the wrong tree grubbing around the backstreets of Calcutta. No one goes there. They're not what I'd call serious players."

Sadly, she chose not to take my advice. Small wonder she died with barely a penny to her name. With her reputation and connections, she could have expected – what? – 250, 300K?

No one likes a little person, be it man or woman. It's a well-known fact that if you're going to be a hard-hitter, you've got to be over 5ft 2ins. And let's not imagine that slogging around in a grubby habit gets you anywhere, either. For all her domestic virtues, Mother Teresa would never have made it to the job of Chief Sub-Editor on a national newspaper.

Lunch is the main job of an editor. Most days, I lunched with high-ranking politicians. I loved those privileged encounters with senior members of the government – men of the calibre of Kenneth Baker.

It was seldom I passed a couple of hours with Ken without at least one indiscretion being yielded. After a particularly heavy meal, I would be able to gauge which way the wind was blowing.

I well remember Ken telling me one day that Douglas thought Willie had tipped the wink to Nigel that Michael had said that Cecil thought Leon had heard something from Margaret about Norman being a serious player. My editor's instinct told me that this was historic news. The very next day, I contributed the following hard-hitting editorial to The Daily Telegraph:

"Governments divide into two categories. The first kind is strong. The second is weak. Weak governments are frankly pathetic. What we need is a strong government – a government that is afraid neither to take a calculated punt at a high bird, nor to dispatch a stag at 20 paces. And this, on present form, is what we have."

My wife and I were lunching alone with Michael Heseltine and his wife, insert name, in early 1997 at his costly stately mansion in Northamptonshire.

We were being served highly-priced food in his Quinlan Terry sun-lounge off hallmarked silver dishes held by his range of liveried well-spoken butlers. You can tell Michael has class: he always removes the price-tags.

The conversation turned to Jeffrey Archer. "Let's face it, Michael," I said, applying the gold Aspreys tongs to the lobster-filled Angus steaks, "the man's nothing but a name-dropping vulgarian – and Andrew Devonshire agrees with me."

A junior butler held the looking-glass steady as Michael dragged a Cartier comb through his extravagant locks.

"There are two kinds of shit," I continued, sagely. "The complete shit – and the prize shit. And Jeffrey is both." Over a very decent Petrus (£350 a bottle wholesale), I gave serious thought to the historic view of shits. "Stalin was a complete shit, Mao a prize shit. John Major's rank of shit we must leave to future historians. But what is beyond doubt is that the man would never listen."

At this point, Mrs Heseltine interrupted with a question. I glanced at my watch. "I can give you two minutes max," I said. While she was boring on about whether anyone would fancy a coffee, I seized the opportunity to pass on a healthy bit of advice. "The world's divided into dogs and grouse," I said, "and it's the dogs that bark, and the grouse that fly. If ever you see a grouse that barks, then, God Almighty, the kindest thing one can do is to wrench its head off. White for me, Mrs H – no sugar, and pretty bloody sharpish."

Joanna Trollope's
Snow White and the Seven Dwarfs

The mirror – that gold-framed, reflective-style looking-glass she had managed to pick up for a bargain £37.00 at the Liberty sale in London's Regent Street the year before last, along with a delicious deep-red throw from Malaya and a sexy little black dress by Gucci which she only ever wore on occasions when she was feeling a bit low and wanted a bit of picking up, as anyone does, these days – was on the wall, in its usual place.

The Queen looked into it, peeringly. It was going to be one of those days, she thought, with a sigh.

"Mirror, mirror on the wall," she began.

"Mm?" intoned the mirror, still on the wall, which it always was. The mirror madly questioned everything. Some considered it cracked.

"Mirror, mirror on the wall," said the Queen, repetitively. She had that looking-in-the-mirror look on her face – a look she invariably put on for looking in the mirror.

The mirror knew, perceived and guessed that the Queen was on edge. Some called her wicked, but she was basically just insecure, experiencing nagging feelings of there's-something-missing, almost as though – in a vague, unspecific, intangible sort of way – there was something missing. She was a victim of the must-do culture of success-at-any-price. If only she'd discuss it!

The mirror desperately wanted to help, desperately wanted to be a shoulder to cry on. But the mirror had problems of her own, goodness she did, problems she wanted to share.

"Mirror, mirror – "

"Putting you through. Bear with me."

"Mirror, mirror on the wall. Who's the fairest of the characters within the remit of those about who I am talking about?"

"Come again?"

The Queen had wanted to ask a simple question. But if life had taught her anything it was that nothing is ever that simple, not when there are so many pages to be got through.

"Well" said the mirror, "it depends what you mean by fairest."

Yes, thought the Queen with a sigh, it was going to be at least three pages before she got anything approaching an answer. She sighed again, and then again. Then once more.

"Men!" thought Snow White, sitting in a highly desirable modern detached house that offered spacious accommodation to up to seven modestly proportioned individuals. "They never discuss their feelings. Instead, they bottle them up, and then things come to the surface and then – well – one thing leads to another".

Too true. These past few weeks, one thing had certainly led to another.

"One thing," she had observed to her best friend, only the other day, before pausing, as though looking for the right combination of words or phrases. But before she had managed to endeavour to try to formulate a suitable ending to the phrase she was about to coin, her best friend Jill – the wife of Bill, who'd tragically fallen out with Phil after he'd left Cill for Will's wife Hil – had finished the sentence for her.

"Leads to another," said her best friend.

"Hm?"

"It... leads to another. One... thing, I mean."

"Yes, I see what you mean, Jill," Snow White had replied in response, adding, additionally, "One thing leads to..."

"Another."

"Tell me, Bashful," said Doc, "why do you whistle while you work?"

"I don't," replied Bashful.

"Denial," retorted Doc, retortingly, "is only ever a coping mechanism."

The two men – neither tall – were having a heart-to-heart. They were each sitting on painted wooden kitchen chairs with four legs, bought in a job-lot just over six years before from an out-of-town antique warehouse that had since gone bust owing to its owner's unfortunate addiction to gambling – an addiction that had cost him his partner, Drusilla, who finally couldn't take it any more and now lived in Guernsey with a retired GP sadly widowed at the end of the 1980s after his second wife Amelia, a former ballet dancer, developed something terminal, with complications.

"Hi ho!" exclaimed Grumpy, entering with a cheery, jolly, merry sort of wave. He'd been so much better since he went on the Prozac.

Doc looked at Grumpy quizzically. "Any news of Dopey?" he asked.

In recent years, Dopey had overcome his earlier learning difficulties by facing up to blockages – emotional and psychological – that were holding him back. As a man, Dopey had failed to keep in touch with his emotions, and for a while they had stopped speaking to him, just to teach him a lesson. But last year he managed to get back in touch with them – it turned out they were living just round the corner in a three-bedroomed house with double garage that must be worth, oooh, roughly half a million pounds, just so long as the council didn't go ahead with the by-pass – and as a result he had achieved a double first in Classics from prestigious, ancient and educational Oxford University, first mentioned as Oxnaforda in the Anglo-Saxon Chronicle as early as 911.

"Hi-ho, guys!" It was Snow White, much happier now that she had come to terms with her childhood trauma, given up smoking and invested in the Estee Lauder range.

Back at the Palace, the Queen tensed herself for an answer. The mirror took a deep breath.

"Snow... White."

"Whatever," sighed the Queen, up-to-dately. She tried to put on a brave face. Now was not the time for recriminations, she thought, thoughtfully. Far better to hook up with Snow White at their local bistro, the picturesque Bella Roma, on the junction of the High Street and Victoria Place, where they did a delicious Chicken Kiev for under ten pounds, wine included, and discuss with her in a thoroughly open and civilised way any deep-seated feelings of low self-esteem either of them may or may not be feeling at the present time. After all, theirs was a contemporary dilemma, and the old-fashioned days of confrontation were over, finished, ended.

Tributes to George Harrison

YOKO ONO

There will never be another George Harrison. How could I forget him? I was married to him for a very long time, and we were always very, very happy together, creating all those lovely songs I wrote with him. Please, I say this to all our fans, don't feel sorry for me now that George has passed on. For he will live in my heart forever, and I own total world rights to his songs. Peel an apricot. Throw it in the air. Here comes the sun. Now the sun has fallen on the ground. It has made a mess. Leave it where it is. Or your hands will become very sticky.

RAY CONNOLLY

I met George Harrison in the autumn of 1966 and this most generous of friends allowed me to talk to him for well over five minutes, possibly almost six.

"Hello, George!" I said, "I'm Ray Connolly!".

"Hi, Ray!" he said. It was as if we had known each other for years. I was never to meet him again, but in that short time, we forged a firm friendship that I was able to spread over the next thirty-three years of articles.

To me, George was always the quietest of The Beatles. And at the same time, he was never the loudest. Looking back, I can see he was very, very quiet indeed. In fact, he said nothing at all to me. I will always remember his response when I asked him whether it was him who played the drums. He just looked at me in a deep and profound silence. As I saw my own image reflected in those deep brown eyes of his, I knew that I was in the presence of a very caring, very loving, very quiet human being.

Incidentally, I met Reg Presley of The Troggs on three separate occasions, and I once shared a good laugh with Chip Hawkes of The Tremeloes. But none of them were as much a part of the Beatles as George. Ah, The Sixties. Magic memories!

MOHAMED FAYED

George Beatle? They fuggin kill him, you know what I telling you, Prince Fuggin Philip and the so-called Queen Mother, that's who, my friend. I never fuggin forgive them, they and their wig-big chums in secret so-called fuggin services, they say, "We got rid Diana, we got rid Kennedy, now we get rid George Fuggin Beatle". My favourite George Beatle song? "Somefugginthing".

FERGAL KEANE

The dew sat heavy, oh so heavy, on the grass. The sun struggled vainly in its battle to lift its head above the clouds groaning in their misery. No, I don't think I shall ever forget the morning I turned on my old Roberts wireless and heard that oh so fateful news.

I write this with the tears dropping – drop, drop, drop – on my typewriter. I listen hard, and I hear them battling to make a tune – drop, drop, drippety-drop, drippety-drop-drop-drop – and I realise with a start that it is one of George's immortal tunes they are trying so desperately to communicate.

George was always my favourite Beatle. To me, he was just like me. And I, in turn, was like him. Sensitive as the cowslips of hope that blossom on the path of our dreams. Spiritual as a smokey fire on a winter's day, its candy-floss plumes drifting up and up and up like angels through the chimney-stack of longing. George, wherever you are, I trust you are reading this, taking real human love and comfort from these mournful words of mine as they flow like tears – the teariest of tears – onto the sad-sodden page.

Piers Morgan
Investigates Fame

Moron: Right now, on this Planet Earth, we are living through nothing less than an explosive tidal wave that's lit a forest fire we simply put into reverse. It amounts to nothing less than a revolutionary hurricane of volcanic proportions. And it's an epidemic that goes by the name of Celebrity.

Beardie Professor 1: In a very real sense, post 9/11, it indicates a seismic shift in the very nature of our culture. As Andy Warhol once said, in fifteen minutes everyone will be famous.

Moron: Everyone now believes they too can be famous for fifteen minutes by appearing on TV. These are sad and deeply troubled individuals with no visible talent. Yet they want to appear on television. Tonight I, Piers Morgan, am appearing on TV to ask them the question – WHY?

Jeremy Clarkson: There's a new breed of celebrity who are designed to be famous for fifteen minutes. All they have is a limitless belief in their own importance. And frankly I – Jeremy Clarkson – feel sorry for them.

Moron: Didn't Andy Warhol say something about being famous for fifteen minutes?

Jeremy Clarkson: Too right he did. He said we'd be famous for fifteen minutes.

Moron: As Andy Warhol once said! But is our obsession with transient celebrity eroding our interest in people with real talent? That's what really concerns me. To find out more about this terrifying new phenomenon, I went to a girl with big tits. Tell me, have you got big tits?

Girl with Big Tits: Yeah. I got big tits. As Andy Warhol once said –

Moron: I'll tell you what deeply worries me. It's that I'm only talking to you on television because you've got big tits. That tells us something literally terrifying about the whole nature of modern celebrity. Tell you what – can we get a close-up on those tits? Great! Fantastic! And if you lean back a bit, they'll look even bigger. Lovely.

Beardie Professor 2: Post 9/11, society's obsession with big tits is indicative of what I believe to be the seismic shift that's occurred in the very nature of our culture.

Moron: The history of celebrity kicks off in 330 BC. Until then, no-one knew who anyone was at all. The world's first fame-seeker was Alexander the Great – and he hit the world of celebrity big-time. Next to be a world-famous megastar was Julius Caesar, later played by Richard Burton, husband to Michael Jackson's close friend, Liz Taylor. As the centuries rolled on, more and more people became celebrities – from leading thinker Plato, to ageing lothario William Shakespeare, from busty babe Nell Gwynne to pocket-size royal Queen Victoria, from mega-boffin Isaac Newton to mega wife-killer Dr Crippen. And so we come to Alicia Douvall, who has bigger tits than the lot of them. So, Alicia, isn't it a bit sad that, post 9/11, we're interviewing you, just because you've got big tits?

Alicia Douvall: I think it was Andy Warhol who said –

Moron: Sorry, love, you couldn't shove them forward a bit, could you? Great!

Beardie Professor 3: A historic rupture occurred causing a seismic shift that signalled a historic decline of confidence in the whole nature of what Andy Warhol historically called –

Alicia Douvall: How's about if I stick my arse out too? Can you fit it all in, can you?

Moron: After Alexander the Great and William Shakespeare came the 1980s, which turned out to be a historic decade. Though I didn't know it at the time, I personally was living through the Eighties. And by the end of that historic decade a completely different type of celebrity had emerged: the famous celebrity.

Paul Morley: The Eighties came immediately after the post-war period but before 9/11, so they occupy a mythic moment in modern thingy, a transforming moment when something truly mythical takes sort of place in a way that can only be described as a transformation into something truly mythic. Or something.

Moron: In 1994 there came a decisive moment in world history, a moment through which I was privileged personally to have lived. Yes, I was here, standing in this exact spot when Liz Hurley first wore That Dress. Overnight, Liz Hurley re-wrote the tidal wave of celebrity using only a safety-pin. And the world would never be the same again. Sadly, Liz was unavailable for interview. But Jordan's tits are much bigger, so what the heck.

Jordan: I'm more than just a pair of boobs, y'know.

Moron: Can we have a close-up on them, guys?

Beardie Professor 4: What we now know as the Hurley phenomenon caused a seismic shift in cultural attitudes towards the very nature of fame itself, as Andy Warhol had so presciently –

Jordan: I had that Mick Hucknall once, you know. Well, he SAID he was Mick Hucknall, bastard. Men! Still, that's life, innit?

Baldie Psychologist: By conforming to society's need to have intercourse with Mick Hucknall, today's celebrities are, in a very real way, seeking to redress an imbalance between their recognitive needs and their associative impulses, resulting in what is technically known as a "seismic shift", leading to a low self-image or, in some cases, accidental death.

Moron: This is a development which, from my point of view as the editor of a serious newspaper, is deeply worrying, as I intend to show with this groundbreaking experiment –

Jordan: It's extra wiv me T-shirt off.

Moron: Post the historic rupture of the Spice Girls and 9/11, an ocean of celebrity wannabes is surging towards us heaping a forest fire of broken dreams on a burst dam of expectations. Should we, as a society, be worried about what Andy Warhol once called our 15-minute fame culture? What is happening to our young? To find out more, we gave 100 sad young folk the once-in-a-lifetime opportunity to look completely desperate on national TV. Next week, I'll be smirking at them behind their backs – and asking top psychologists just what it's like, historically, to have tits as big as Jordan's.

Robert Hughes's 6 Greatest Artists of All Time

CHARDIN

At the tender age of 15, I was as horny as a blue-arsed fly and bursting out of my 33% cotton underpants, bought by my mother in packs of three at a prestigious Melbourne department store. And then I set eyes on a still life by Chardin. At fifteen, to find this voice – so finely wrought and yet so raw, public and yet strangely private – speaking to me with such insistence and urgency from a remote time and a country I'd never been to, of whose language I spoke not a word, was no small thing.

It was an orange on which I looked that precious dew-dropped morn, and it was instantly recognisable as such. But anyone who thinks it was just an orange knows nothing, neither of oranges nor Chardin. Indeed, such a total ignoramus would be the kind of slimebag who would rate Corot above Courbet, or who would have the sheer bloody nerve to suggest that Churchill was a greater war leader than Chamberlain, just as some right-wing loonies in America still believe in the existence of God, a tomfool creed that I shed along with my short trousers in adolescence, an awakening enlightenment for which I count myself grateful.

GOYA

It would, perforce, be an utter and outright nerd who dared to suggest that the twentieth century, that atrocious epoch of failed dreams and trumphant death, did not have one or two consolations of which, I would modestly attest, I am not the least.

But though the eighteenth century gave birth to its fair share of gormless lickspittles and sundry jerks (the spineless fat-arsed creep Reynolds, the berk Burke), it also had the good fortune to deliver Francisco Goya, not only a truly extraordinary artist but – and I say this with all possible urgency not to say another word like urgency – an artist extraordinaire.

It was to Goya's great good fortune that, some two and a half centuries after the year appertaining to his birth, he at last found his true and natural biographer, namely myself. He was, I suspect, drawn to me not only for my depth but also for my width. And anyone who could presume to suggest Goya was in any way disappointed with his biographer must be a bigger moron than even his worst enemy – and believe me, son, you have a great many of that species – could possibly imagine.

MONET

There isn't any evidence that Monet was interested in water-lilies, as lacklustre critics have suggested in the past. Far from it. Like Alan Titchmarsh in the present day, the guy was infinitely more interested in the herbaceous border, so colourful yet so verdant, and rightly so. Agreed, he painted those soppy and sopping oblong flowers as they jammed up his ponds, but it can't possibly have been because he saw any worth in the things. Believe me, he was no fool. So why did he bother with those damned water-lilies? An informed guess tells me they reminded him of the voluptuous arse of a female aborigine – only in these politically-correct times the spineless and the lily-livered are happy to bow to the demands of the thought police and cover up this fact.

VELAZQUEZ

The guy was one of the most dedicated snobs that ever touched a brush. But that should not take anything away from his quite magnificent achievement. Looking at a canvas by Velazquez, I am literally overcome by the knowledge that here is an artist about whom no words of mine could pay tribute either adequate or inadequate. So how to face up to the challenge and put into words the effect this truly incomparable painter has on those to whom he not only speaks but paints?

Like most if not all of Velazquez's incomparable paintings, I am well hung, and like every red-blooded male I have always found the dwarf pictured near the front of the painting in Las Meninas powerfully erotic. Put it like this. It is not hard to imagine pulling off her unexceptional gown and giving her a powerful seeing-to, possibly in the bedchamber of her mistress, and, ideally, in the energetic company of the gagging-for-it Rokeby Venus (to my mind infinitely sexier than our own contemporary, Pamela Anderson, who, though commendably curvaceous, albeit in a manner that might strike the connoisseur as a little too glaringly upfront, has nevertheless the undeniable qualities of generous fleshiness, notwithstanding roughly applied brushwork.

WHISTLER

And the same allure – mysterious, and also, in a curious way, full of mystery – undoubtedly applies to Whistler's mother, a lady of a certain age whose powerful physical charms are rampantly obvious to any fellow still halfway capable of showing a girl a good time between the sheets.

What were the thoughts of Whistler (history teaches us the guy couldn't whistle for toffee, incidentally) as he grasped that brush and, bold as brass, began to paint his somewhat buttoned-up mother? What sort of lurid, lascivious and sexually charged thoughts lurked in the painterly mind of this distinguished Massachusetts-born painter who was influenced by Courbet, irritated Ruskin, sometime art-critic, genius and thoroughgoing drip, and whose work bears the unmistakable imprint of both Fantin-Latour and the Japanese masters, as he stared like a certifiable perve at his mother, his mum, the woman who gave him birth?

Did he stare hard, attempting to trace the slender curve of her implausibly perky breasts, so vibrant yet so still, and the delicate thrust of her come-hither buttocks as he slapped those first few strokes of bluey-grey on the well-primed canvas? We do not know, and only a slobbering old man would dare ask such an impertinent, unreasonable and objectionable question. But on the available evidence, scant as it may be, there is no reason to doubt he fancied her something rotten.

REMBRANDT

I've been writing about Rembrandt for thirty-odd years. For this, he has good cause to be grateful. Others don't get the hots for those murky browns and detect a certain shiftiness about the eyes in those self-portraits, so curiously revealing yet so strangely unrevealing. But thirty years of shitting my guts out on his behalf has paid off. Rembrandt's now taken seriously as an artist, thanks to me, and I intend to write a book to give an overdue leg-up to bald 16th century playwright Shakespeare, whom I rate very highly, and who gives a shit what my enemies think, dammit.

Lady Annabel Goldsmith

I was wearing a rather low-cut bathing suit which displayed my bosom to maximum advantage! It was unconventional in those days to wear a rather low-cut bathing suit to a formal dinner-party! But then I have always been a rather unconventional sort of woman!

Needless to say, the eyes of the men at the table were literally glued to my cleavage! So I decided to divert their attention by insisting on a round of silly games!

"I know what!" I shrieked, delightedly, "Let's play hunt the thimble!"

And with that I withdrew into the sitting-room, and got darling Mrs Stokes, who once cooked her perfect sherry trifle for Adolf Eichmann, to place a thimble down what many have been kind enough to describe as my remarkable cleavage!

"Hunt the thimble – ready, steady, go!" I whooped as I returned to the dining-room! In fact, I tried to make it easier for them by pointing at the likely area! But sadly not one of the gentlemen looked up, thank you very much!

On closer investigation, I discovered they were otherwise engaged in plopping their "members" (how I hate that word!) on the table to see whose was the largest!

Then they all got out their felt-tips, painted funny faces on them and re-enacted the Battle of Omdurman! "I know when I'm not wanted, gents!" I exclaimed, good-heartedly dipping into my own bosom for my thimble and retreating upstairs for an early night with something milky and a copy of the latest *Vogue*!

In those heady, far-off days, we certainly knew how to have fun! My grandmother, Edith, the seventh Marchioness of Londonderry taught me how! She had always been intent on injecting gaiety into life!

Her charmed circle would gossip like mad, play silly games, flirt with each other, tell outrageous jokes, widdle down the stairwell, and drink copious quantities of the delicious pre-war Londonderry champagne!

She even enjoyed a close friendship with the Labour leader Ramsay MacDonald! "He was an old-fashioned socialist," she wrote in her memoirs. "He loved beautiful things, gorgeous pageantry, fine silverware, dressing up in resplendent uniforms, being waited on hand and foot, and taking the cream of the British aristocracy up the arse!"

Throughout my life, we couldn't have had half so much fun without our full complement of servants, all of them the most tremendous characters!

The marvellous thing was how much they respected us! I'll never forget what the inimitable Mr Chambers, Daddy's bathroom butler, said after vigorously wiping Daddy's behind after he had experienced a particularly severe dose of diarrhoea!

He said, "It's come up beautiful, sir – and may I add what a pleasure and a privilege it has been for me to attend to you today!"

Sadly, Mr Chambers shot himself the next day. It could have been the most frightful blow, but thankfully the vacancy was soon filled!

When I first set eyes on Jimmy Goldsmith, I fell madly in love with him!

There was a simplicity about the way he would draw great bundles of notes out of his top pocket in a single movement that I found wholly irresistible!

Despite his debonair image, Jimmy preferred the simple things in life! His absolute favourite thing in the world was a simple boiled egg in bed, served by members of his junior airstaff in his simple private jet!

And he was simply marvellous with people! With a simple punch to the ribs, followed by a swift jab on the nose, he could always get them to do just what he wanted!

I'll never forget the time we met the famous Nelson Mandela, who – much to our surprise! – was black! I was helpless with laughter! But Jimmy was a businessman through and through, and he certainly wasn't going to mess up a contract by making a fuss about it!

I was wearing a low-cut night-dress at the time, and I noticed how much time Nelson spent pretending not to stare at my world-famous cleavage!

With his quick wit, Jimmy came straight to the point! "Oh, for fuck's sake, the man's a bloody nigger!" he erupted, banging a nearby table lightheartedly with his fist!

"Welcome to our country," said Nelly in that funny voice of his! By this time, I was almost weeing myself with laughter! But then I've always been unconventional!

"Call this a fucking country?!" replied Jimmy, quick as a flash,

"It's more like a shit-hole! But I'll buy it anyway!"

Jimmy was always the most enormous fun!

Friends often ask me what it's like to have a nightclub named after one! I tell them that frankly I don't know what it would be like not to have a nightclub named after one!

Annabel's has always attracted the most amazing characters! "Lucky" Lucan would often drop by, and he would often peer at my bosoms!

But then he killed his nanny accidentally on purpose – and suddenly stopped coming!

Nicky van Hoogstraaten was always enormously entertaining, with the most perfectly shined shoes you could imagine! I always enjoyed a dance with Armand Hammer when he was in town – even if I did notice his hands down my cleavage from time to time! I was once sorely tempted to tell him off – but Jimmy said don't be such a fucking spoilsport or you'll jeopardise the fucking deal!

You see, beneath it all, Jimmy was always so very vulnerable!

Another great character was John Aspinall! Aspers lost heaven knows how many keepers to his wild animals over the years, poor things! Aspers had the most perfect manners, and would always make the most tremendous point of apologising to their next of kin, if any! And nor would he charge the family for the loss of uniform! That's the kind of man he was!

I once took a party of underprivileged children to Aspers' zoo and – against my better judgement! – shut them all in the lions' cage while I nipped off to change into something more revealing! When I got back, there were only a few half-chewed socks and sandals left – and, goodness, I felt awful! But Jimmy insisted there's nothing any of us can do about the problems of the underprivileged! And at least the lions were able to enjoy a well-earned zizz!

David Starkey: The True Story of the Nativity

Christina Rossetti claimed it all happened in the deep mid-winter, and she managed to rake in a small fortune for her efforts, thank you very much.

Snow on snow, eh? Well, pants to her, say I.

There's not the mimsiest peck of evidence that the Nativity occured in mid-winter, deep or otherwise. Well, that's women for you – no sense of time and incapable of holding the smallest fact in their silly little heads! Typical!

So let's aim for a bit of accuracy in our history, shall we, ladies?

FACT: In the fields, the shepherds were tending their sheep. They were rough, tough men, ever so burly, and with filthy-dirty hands. If one had so much as *offered* them a bar of Lifebuoy, they would have run an absolute mile. They were educated at the

School of Hard Knocks, followed by a degree course at the University of Life. But they learnt quite enough to take to the fields of a starry night rather than suffer their wives' incessant scolding and nattering over the kitchen stove.

So there these fine figures of shepherds are – out in those blessed fields, perhaps comparing muscles or arm-wrestling, or rubbing one another down with grass-based oils or engaging in the most wicked sort of shepherdy gossip when – hark! – the herald angel sings. "Glory to the new-born king!"

Come again?

Talk about ancient photo-opportunities! So who exactly WAS this buxom herald angel – and what exactly did she intend by her *ghastly* womanly caterwauling?

Those intelligent enough to have understood my internationally-acclaimed scholarly work "NATIVITY: The Roller-Coaster Life of the Herald Angel" (OUP), soon to be made into a four-part television series for which I received a very handsome advance, thank you very much (well into six figures, since you ask), will already know that – and here I quote from leading expert myself – "Like most members of the female species, she was part wench, part nag. With her showy wings and come-hither smile, she was the ultimate power-dresser, destined to make mincemeat of any man – be he king or shepherd – who stood in her way".

Such vim and gusto in one's prose! This is the way to bring history alive. Why do lesser historians (my so-called "rivals" – I ask you!) go out of their way to make everything so deadly dreary? With a few flicks – flick! flick! flick! – of my pen, I bring history to life, making it accessible to that unspeakable specimen, the man on the Clapham Omnibus, to say nothing of his young friend sitting next to him.

Off the poor shepherds dutifully set, simply *livid* to be wrenched from their manly labours by this cheap little hussy smothered in too much lipstick and swamped by a gallon of mascara. Meanwhile, in another corner of the world, three Kings sat a-swooning in their gorgeous finery.

Of course, that fashionable band of "revisionist" historians – blessed with the happy coincidence that they understand the past better than those of us who have engaged in a lifetime's study – may claim that these three kings wore the tedious modern-day uniform of grubby jeans and t-shirt. But what, may one ask, do THEY know? They're paid a pittance, and if you pay chicken-feed you get chickens. Doesn't it positively make you want to vomit?

Compare MY earnings for the past fiscal year with those of my rivals!

In real terms, I pocketed considerably more than A.J.P. Taylor, not to mention toffee-nosed Lord Kenny Clark, who was barely paid enough to keep him in monocles. And as for Mr Simon Bloody Schama in his open-necked terylenes and *hideous* blouson jackets, his most recent audience figures have proved deeply disappointing, confirmation that he simply doesn't have the popular appeal to command the highest rates in future.

So by my calculations – officially confirmed by my team of top accountants – I am now the biggest grossing historian the world has ever known. Only last week, the Daily Express offered me a cool £2500 for 800 words on Why Jonny Wilkinson Is Just So Utterly Butterly, and I managed to write it in 25 minutes flat, memorably describing him as the Oliver Cromwell of his day (or was it the Charles I?).

But – smacky bottys, David! – I digress. The scene now switches to the manger, the Baby Jesus looking *most* uncomfortable – after all, who could *possibly* look good in *swaddling* clothes, I ask you?! History does not record what went through that little head of his, but of one thing you can be sure:

he was sick to the back teeth with the way those cattle wouldn't stop their lowing, and simply couldn't *wait* for the touch of seasonal glamour provided by a visit from three kings.

His hangdog stepfather Joseph was a two-bit carpenter of little or no interest to anyone. There is only so much fascination to be had from a shelving unit. The child's mother, Mary, for all her airs and graces, was no better than she should have been. Little Miss Perfect I don't think. And it didn't stop her getting in the family way, now, did it?

Between the two of them, they presented a sorry sight. Their feel for home furnishings was *pitiful*, and, with donkeys, sheep and heaven-knows-what scattered all over the place, one quite *blanches* at the absence of hygiene.

For all their tedious do-goodery, this grim couple did nothing to merit a visit from one king, let alone all *three*! Small wonder the regal threesome didn't waste a minute in that sordid stable before depositing their gifts and bidding their goodbyes. Wise men indeed. Memo to Mary and Joseph: I myself was twice invited to dine at Kensington Palace with the late HRH Princess Margaret, and only recently I stayed with Darling Debo at Chatsworth.

Touché!

So we leave them there in the stable, all alone now that the kings have scarpered and the shepherds have (finally!) cleared off. What does the future hold for the Infant Jesus? Well, he certainly wasn't backward in coming forward was he? But for all his fame (largely posthumous, I might add), he earned a fraction of what I earn – AND he never made the cover of the TV Times.

Matthew Freud's
Wedding Diary

For me – and here I'm speaking on behalf of Elizabeth too – marriage continues to be a superbly productive cross-fertilisation of mutual client interests, endorsed by God, who, I'm delighted to say, joined us last week.

As my client Chris Evans confirmed in a press release last Wednesday, God is – and I quote – "the numero uno, the King Pin, the ultimate Mr Fixit, Elvis, Geri Halliwell, Britvic and the new Braun Oral B3 Excel electric toothbrush all rolled into one".

Thanks for that consummately professional, very positive product boost, Chris! So it seemed like an obvious piece of casting to bring Him right into the mega-centre of the bigger picture when it came to joining M. Freud and E. Murdoch in Holy Wedlock!

(Incidentally, you can find out a whole lot more about our

hugely successful record-breaking wedding last Saturday
by clicking onto our exclusive new marito-website, www.freud-
murdoch@pepsi.com)

My exclusive bride Elizabeth – powerful, super-sexy daughter
of top international media mogul Rupert Murdoch – woke to a
brilliantly sunny Oxfordshire-style morning in our superb multi-
million-pound 12-bedroom executive-style home in the grounds
of exclusive Blenheim Palace, impressive as a cool, refreshing
bottle of Holsten Pils. Fan-tastic! No, it wasn't raining at all! Not a
bit! Okay, so who told you it was raining? I said, who told you? If
you're not going to tell me who the fuck spread these fucking
lies, I'm going to terminate this diary right now. Okay, that's it.
You're dead meat, my friend. Let me remind you I'm lunching
with your boss on the 24th.

Great! Fab! Good man! So it was a sensationally sunny
Barbados-style morning in the grounds of world-famous
Blenheim Palace WITHOUT A DROP OF RAIN. I turned to my
future wife, Elizabeth, brilliantly successful daughter of the 39th
richest man in the world, and said, "Today's the day when our
high expectations for a successful world-class wedding launch are
going to be exceeded in every respect." I then offered to get her
a cup of refreshing coffee, recommending Nescafe Gold
Blend for a smoother, richer taste. "Mmmmm... fuller-flavour
coffee granules – that sounds like my kind of coffee," she
replied.

I looked at her with an expression of deepest, pre-marital
love. "You're as beautiful as top breakfast TV presenter Cat
Deeley – and as appealing as the new range of Scantihose, now
available at leading branches of the totally re-energised and
world-beating M&S fashion superstore," I said, powerfully.

We hired a top-rated vicar for the wedding. He'd given me a bell earlier to make the arrangements. "I can give you precisely three minutes thirty," I said to him, accommodatingly.

He ran me through the service – introduction, prayer, blessing, blah, blah, blah, end. "I'm going to have to interrupt you there," I said. "We need at least two mentions of the new Volkswagen Golf – as driven by Ryan Giggs to the 7-Up-sponsored post-premiere VIP party for the new Bruce Willis movie at Planet Hollywood."

The vicar looked blank. "Look, you're potentially the world's top vicar," I explained. "Stick with me, and I can make your career go mega-stratospheric. You want to be Chief Rabbi? Archbishop of Canterbugs? Pope? Whatever? No prob! At the moment, you're serving God. Well, that's all right for a month or two, but by December I want that vice-versa, get it?

"But first, you'll have to be a nice little vicar and do what I fucking say, okay? So it's the new VW Golf, Giggsie, 7-Up, Bruce Willis and Planet Hollywood IN THAT ORDER, okay? Cheers, mate!"

It turned out to be a superb wedding, delivering a prestige fast-track service targeting some of the most highly-placed VIPs on the planet, all packed into the same high-profile church. The vicar sported Lynx aftershave, new from the exclusive toiletries for men range at Boots. Anneka Rice, whose career, let me tell you, is destined for a massive remake, introduced the service with an excellent selection of in-house videos portraying Elizabeth – super-successful daughter of media tycoon Rupert Murdoch – and myself as a very positive, very today, very caring-but-go-getting sort of couple. Then instead of the usual draggy hymns, we successfully placed a selection of new songs by Cat Deeley, who looks set to be huge, followed by a very quiet, very real, very spiritual element – the Gospel sponsored by Chicken Tonight read as you've never heard it read before by those totally manic mischief-makers Ant and Dec.

A VIP communion was served by Uri Geller, with two cans of Pepsi Blue given away free with every wafer. Accompanying music was by the one and only Geri Halliwell, who treated all guests to presentation copies of her all-new Workout Video. It was our aim to create a relaxed yet wholly energised atmosphere in which people could hang out and exchange product ideas in an easy-going, hi-density, world-class, religious-yet-not-too-religious environment. And then came the biggie.

"Do you, Matthew Freud of Freud Communications, take Elizabeth Murdoch, daughter of mega-powerful media moghul Rupert Murdoch, to be your lawfully wedded wife?" asked the top international vicar, tipped for great things.

"I'll get back to you soonest," I said, punching out a number on my Nokia 425 All-Weather Mobile to confirm with KissFM that they'd come in with Dolce e Gabbana on the exclusive VIP after-nuptials bash.

I then got back to the vicar. "Sorted," I said – and so ended the wedding of the century, termed by all the top media pundits as a marriage made in heaven*.

---

* Heaven is a copyright product of Chessington World of Adventures incorporating Jiffi Condoms, a wholly-owned subsidiary of News International.

Christopher Ricks

Warren Professor of the Humanities at Boston University and formerly King Edward VII Professor of English Literature at the University of Cambridge

on Sir Cliff Richard's Visions of Sin

Cliff – a word at once reassuring yet perilous. A bird – a seagull, a hawk – sits atop the Cliff. Is he ready to fly, or will he fall instead with a flap and a screech to his death?

Sir Cliff (or is it sur cliff, for he is now, more than ever, surely on that cliff) has always had a way with words. He does not simply have his way with them, since a true comprehender of words is no more their master than he or she is their servant. The triangle of Richard's music, his voices, and his unpropitiatory words: this is still his equilateral thinking.

> *Congratulations and celebrations*
> *When I tell everyone that you're in love with me.*
> *Congratulations and jubilations*
> *I want the world to know I'm happy as can be.*

Am I alone in detecting an underlying note of sadness, of melancholy, of extreme and nightmarish desolation, in Cliff's signature tune? He states, maintains, avers, that he wants "the world" to know that he is as "happy as can be". But the tone is brutally ironic, as if in morbid acknowledgement, like T.S. Eliot before him, that his is an ambition that is wholly unattainable, for the fast-moving world (whirled?) is too preoccupied with its own thoughts, actions and consequences to concentrate on the state of mind, happy or otherwise, of Sir Cliff Richard.

———————

Congratulations – and celebrations. The hard 'c' of congratulations clashes against the sibillant soft 'c' of celebrations (a name also given to a luxury selection of chocolates formed, tellingly, of centres both hard and soft – my own preference, incidentally, is for the soft, particularly the strawberry creme) like a knife through silk. The effect of emotional uneasiness is both maintained and reinforced by his devastating employment of words beginning with 'w' – when, want, world – in the second and fourth lines.

These 'w' words (and the word "word" is, don't forget, itself a word beginning with 'w') carry echoes of the sadness inherent in words like woe, weep and wail: in these lines Richard is evidently semaphoring his own turbulent state of mind, by turns desperate for the acclaim of the entire world population for his struggle towards happiness ("I want the world to know...") yet at the same time poignantly aware that his contentment is only relative ("I'm as happy as can be") to his own, perhaps even greater, capacity for a bitter and brooding unhappiness.

In the third line, "jubilations" , with all its Old Testament echoes of judgement and retribution, rhymes – precisely, uncannily, and with uncanny precision – with the "congratulations" of the title. And there is undeniable sexual tension, too, in Richard's prolonged rendition of the "lay" in jubiLAYtions and "congratuLAYtions" when set against the emphatically standoffish "shun" of jubilaSHUNs and congratulaSHUNs. Seduction versus rejection: it is the greatest artists who take risks, and what could be riskier for Cliff than to bare his deepest sexual misgivings with such purgatory bravado?

The enigma behind the enigma. Interviewed by Michael Parkinson in September, 1974, Sir Cliff Richard made one of the most revelatory comments of his entire career as a poet: "That's right, Michael, I guess I'd have to say I've had a truly great time making this latest album."

At first glance, the words are deceptively simple. But, as so often with Richard, they carry the inescapable acknowledgement that the inexpressible must defy – or define, or even deify – expression. "Great" can also be spelt "grate". Thus Richard was, once again, sending out a message of heartfelt despair beneath his familiar and terrifyingly transparent guise of cautious geniality.

This note of disillusion with the world comes to a head in his fierce, scabrously cynical (not to say sin-ical) and unyieldingly angry "Mistletoe and Wine" (December 1988).

> *Christmas time, mistletoe and wine*
> *Children singing Christian rhyme*
> *With logs on the fire and gifts on the tree*
> *A time for rejoicing in all that we see.*

Some have taken this lyric at surface value (is there ever any value in surface?) arguing that it is in some way a "hymn to the joy of Christmas". But the very word "hymn" is, please note, just one diminutive vowel away from "hymen", which is itself, of course, an aural doppelganger of "Hi, men!"

The rhyming scheme seems at first simple – a-a-b-b – but then you notice Richard's intense frustration in attempting to rhyme "rhyme" with "wine". By employing an unworkable rhyme – ("wine") to rhyme with "rhyme" – he successfully undermines the very foundations of verse, and by doing so implies that the traditional fabric of Christmas itself is nothing more than a sentimental illusion, allusion and elusion. Sir Cliff's plan is both wild and cunning: once he has prepared his Biblical den of iniquity ("mistletoe and wine") he will throw logs, gifts and trees on the fire and begin his saturnalian debauchery, inviting other males in to deflower virgins.

Richard's indebtedness to William Blake, T.S. Eliot and F. Pontin is further evidenced in the plangent, pungent (and, I, too, am a pun gent) poetry of "Summer Holiday" (1963).

Here, Cliff once again expresses his metaphysical belief in going, like Henry Vaughan, to "where the sun shines brightly" and where, furthermore, "the sea is blue". But his yearning is double-edged, double-crossed, double-decker, double-scotch, double-dutch: for he then adds, bitterly and bittily, "we've seen it in the movies. Now let's see if it's true."

The illusion of the movies can never counterbalance the gruesome – I grew some, too, in my day – reality of the attained holiday. "Doing things we always wanted to... To make our dreams come true." In an extraordinarily beautiful act of artistic compression, Richard rhymes "to" with "true", leaving the darker rhymes – boo, sue, screw, poo – to fester in the reader's mind, like cabbage in a larder. The question is posed, and then unposed: but Sir Cliff has never been angrier.

Ben Elton

Hey, baby, baby, ba-a-a-by – let's ROCK!

Magic words. Truly magical, magic words.

And that's the truly wonderful solid-gold hey-guys-let's-get-up-'n'-boogie true spirit of rock 'n' roll I'm aiming to capture in "We Will We Will Rock You!", the new mega-musical I've written with and about the legendary collective genius that is Queen.

But don't get me wrong. When I employ the word "baby" in this context, I have no intention whatever of using the word in a derogatory or demeaning sense, or as any sort of sexist put-down of the female of the species, for whom I have and will continue to have the very greatest respect.

"Baby" is merely the term I use to conjure up the wondrous innocence of a bygone age – not that I think that this particular bygone age was necessarily innocent, or that the world has not progressed in terms of tolerance, social equality and mutual respect since those dark days in the 1950s of food rationing, tuberculosis and Conservative rule.

Not that I am criticising those who choose to use "baby" in this sense, I hasten to add. That is purely a matter for them and their consciences. And please let's not forget that "baby" also means a very, very young child.

And I'm going to stick my neck out here and tell you something I believe in most definitely: *no single creature on this crazy war-torn planet is as beautiful or as innocent as a new-born baby child.*

Rock and pop has always been a big part of my life. And for breadth, depth, scale and sheer unadulterated joy, to my mind nothing beats the sheer magic that is Queen.

There are so many solid gold Queen hits to chose from. Bohemian Rhapsody. Another One Bites the Dust. Radio Gaga. Bohemian Rhapsody. Another One Bites the Dust. Bohemian Rhapsody. Radio Gaga. And – to my mind perhaps greatest of all – the immortal Bohemian Rhapsody.

Truly classic sounds, loved by men and women of all races the world over. And – blimey O'Riley – (no offence to my very good friends the Irish people, who have already suffered one helluva lot during their long and chequered history) what totally unforgettable lyrics!

> *"Scaramouche, Scaramouche, will you do the fandango*
> *Thunderbolt and lightning – very very frightening me*
> *Oh me, oh me, oh meeeeeeeeeeeeeeeee*
> *Galileo, Galileo, Galileo, Galileo*
> *I will not let you go, let me go, I will not let you go, let me go,*
> *I will not let you go, let me go, I will not let you go, let me go,*
> *go, go"*

These lyrics belong to all of us. They are part of our life

stories. People know them like they know their own mothers. And I have the greatest of respect for all mothers, who do a hell of a difficult job under truly difficult circumstances for little if any reward. They may not always know what these lyrics are about, but they know they mean something, even if it is something they don't know the meaning of, because the words mean different things to different people at different times, or indeed nothing at all to anyone at any time. And that, my friend, is their genius.

———————————

How to turn this solid gold work of genius into a dazzling[1] rockin' and rollin' new musical? Believe me, I grappled with the sheer immensity of this problem for many, many minutes before coming up with the solution. "We Will We Will Rock You!" is a futuristic fantasy, an epic battle between a group of rebels and the forces of pop homogenisation that have come to dominate the planet.

I know what you're gonna think. You're gonna think it is an attack on the fashion for manufactured pop. Natch. Well, I respect your right to think that, but the simple fact is that it is not – though it does, I hope, contain pertinent though well-intentioned and hopefully constructive criticism of some minor aspects of the music business.

I have always maintained that satire is at its best when it is able to celebrate its target, to take the broader view and say, "Hey, perhaps it's not one hundred and one per cent perfect – but,

———————————

1 Though the new musical employs a truly fabulous light show, I would like to stress at this point I have no wish to further endanger the already dangerously depleting levels of energy on this or any other planet through reckless over-use of electricity and lightbulbs. For this reason, I have tried to keep the show's dazzle to a basic minimum, whilst bearing in mind the quite justified expectations of a West End audience (or any other audience, for that matter – please let's never forget that a great many hardworking folk live many, many hundreds of miles from the centre of London, and will only be able to get to the show when it tours closer to their own, often severely under-resourced, localities, bless them).

c'mon, guys, it's pretty damn good all the same!"

Looking back, this is what my youthful "attacks" on La Thatch were all about. I didn't approve of the lady's politics – no way, José![2] But I had a great deal of respect for the way she struggled against the largely male establishment – and often, mind, against our old friend (or rather enemy!) the forces of globalisation – to release this country from the stranglehold of union rule and high taxes, and to liberate solid gold creative talents such as the mighty Lloyd Webber who were not afraid to test their worth in the marketplace. So, no, my political position has not changed since my Thatch-bashing days – and I will continue to slag off, in my own inimitable way(!), those who try to undermine the spirit of free enterprise in this once-great country of ours. That's 'nuff political gear for now, friends – let's boogie!

Kylie Minogue – great entertainer. The Spice Girls – a truly legendary conglomeration of talents. Pete Waterman – the guy's a legend. Gareth Gates – there'll always be a valued place in Pop Music for a young man of his undoubted ability. By celebrating the towering Shakespearian achievements of the four brilliant and uncompromising artistes who were – and will always be – Queen, I am not intending to diss the rest. So, friends, let's raise a glass[3] to everyone in the music industry – and let's ROCK!

---

2 This colloquialism is in no way intended as a slight on the Spanish, or Latin-American community, whose many notable achievements have my total respect, Pinochet and his murderous henchmen excluded.

3 Alcohol can indeed be pleasurable if consumed in moderation. Having said that, I will continue to exercise very great respect for those in the teetotal and alcoholic communities.

Mary Archer

Jeffrey Archer, to whom, as is already widely known, I am married, is permitted by the authorities to come home for Sunday lunch every other week. Colleagues and close acquaintances ask how I can possibly cope with seeing so much of him. I respond by saying that, yes, it is a tremendous ordeal, of course it is, but it is an ordeal through which we must somehow get.

I'm sorry, but that's all I want to say on this particular subject.

My preparations for Jeffrey's fortnightly return are indeed extensive, not to say arduous. A few days before, I generally telephone one or two of his former Conservative colleagues. I extend to them an invitation to join us. They inform me they are sadly unavailable owing to pressure of retirement.

"Anyone coming?" asks Jeffrey, excitedly, on the prison telephone.

"Fortunately, Jeffrey, they have all insisted we take a breather this weekend!" I exclaim. In the peculiar situation within which we find ourselves, it is as well to remain positive.

"Fair enough," says Jeffrey. "But why not put their names in our appointments diary anyway? Margaret and Denis, John and Norma, and let's add a bit of razzle dazzle with the Lloyd Webbers. Tremendous!"

Jeffrey remains in good spirits. I insert their names in the diary, and add that of President George W. Bush and his wife, who are close friends. On Jeffrey's instructions I may also lay places for them, just in case. It goes without saying that falsifying one's Sunday lunch guest list is perfectly normal practice in most healthy marriages. I'm sorry, but that is all I am prepared to say on that subject at this juncture.

It is an undeniable feature of contemporary life that those who wish to cook Sunday lunch must first pay a visit to the shops in order to observe the ingredients, with a view to purchase.

First, I visit the butcher. Inconveniently, there are other people before me in the queue. I look at their blank, bored faces and think to myself, "They may be first in the queue, but do these resolutely ordinary people have interesting thoughts going on in their heads?"

I permit myself a discreet smile. As the Chairman of the Lloyds Hardship Committee, I was in touch – not literally of course – with a great many ordinary people. I need no lessons in how to deal with them, thank you very much.

"Good morning, Lady Archer," says the butcher, somewhat abruptly. "And how are you today?"

"Quite well," I reply. "However, I am not here to exchange banter, but rather to purchase raw meat for my husband's return.

Let us apply our minds to the matter in hand. And that is all I am prepared to say on the subject."

I am fully aware that there is a perception of me as emotionally cold and perhaps rather arrogant. Utter nonsense, of course, and I have nothing but contempt for the sadly rather dull little people who make the suggestion. I feel things quite as much, or as little, as the next person. But I have no wish to make a public song-and-dance of my emotions.

I have known loss and pain, my goodness I have. Many years ago, after my husband made a silly mistake and we were cheated out of our fortune, I was forced to give up our well-equipped seven-bedroom house in The Boltons. More recently, I had to cancel our annual garden party owing to Jeffrey's absence.

In both cases, the pain was all too real. Yet some people, I'm sorry, I'm not going to deign to name them, some people continue to insist that I am emotionally 'cold'. For these people, I hold nothing but contempt.

On the way home, I enter the greengrocer's shop. What must it be like to serve fruit and vegetables all day, every day? One does feel for these people, of course one does. For this reason, if for no other, they are among my portfolio of interests. It is not their fault, or at least not entirely, that it is not for them to attain the intellectual abilities accorded to the rest of us. "Good morning," I say as I hand the greengrocer my shopping list. I simultaneously award him a brief smile. It is the least one can do.

"Anything else, your ladyship?" says the greengrocer when he has at long last finished packing everything up for one. His remark frankly surprises me.

"I have no recollection of requesting anything else," I say, firmly. By the look on his face, I can see that he acknowledges, however ruefully, the truth of my observation.

Sunday, mid-day. The house is temporarily disturbed as Jeffrey arrives home for lunch. "Hello," I say, a form of greeting I have long found helpful if not wholly necessary within the boundaries of a legal marriage.

Jeffrey's trial and subsequent imprisonment were both highly irksome. Anyone who sat through that trial knew that Jeffrey was not lying. Look at the court records. They conclusively prove that Jeffrey never spoke in his own defence. And let me make it quite clear that Jeffrey has never, ever lied without speaking.

Nor has anyone ever doubted my own version of events. They know better than to do that. I am, among other things, the Chairman of the Ethics Committee at Addenbrookes Hospital, and well used to coming down hard on those who lie incompetently. Life has taught me that the truth is all very well in its place, though people of intelligence may well find it insufficient.

"Delicious meal, Mary! Absolutely marvellous!" says Jeffrey, putting a slice of cooked chicken into his mouth. I glance at my watch.

"Oh dear," I say. "I'm afraid your car will be here for you in an hour and a half. And just when you were enjoying yourself!"

I let him chat away in the kitchen while I go outside and give the roses my full attention. I'm very English like that! I then get him to stand in the drive, say my goodbyes and close the door. There's forty minutes until the car comes for him. But better safe than sorry.

Sir Peregrine Worsthorne:
In Defence of Aristocracy

I do not think I am exaggerating when I say that the English
aristocracy has given birth to all the world's greatest and noblest
minds, men without whose breeding and intelligence the human
race would still be splashing about in some ghastly over-heated
swamp in the very belly of darkest Africa as ill-shod toads[1], peevish
lizards or vulgar jelly-fish.

I know that whereof I speak, for I was myself born into the
very bosom of the aristocracy. As is well-known in aristocratic
circles, my great-grandmother's second husband had a third
cousin who was an Anstruther of Godalming. The Anstruthers
stand as the veriest beacons of the hereditary principle, having

---

1 The natterjack toad, an ancestor of the Earl and Countess of Natterjack, is the exception
that proves the rule, being exceedingly good company, an animal of proven nobility, both
genetic and moral, and a member of White's.

given over their lives to looking after the people of Godalming, supplying them with nutritious scraps in cold spells and taking them to court only when the subsequent bills have remained unpaid.

I have often heard it said, and sometimes within earshot of the upper echelons of respectable society, that two and two make four. Yet this is quite plainly not the case. How could two and two possibly make four when it is so obvious to one and all that they make six? To put it simply, if I have two snuff boxes in my left hand, and two snuff boxes in my right hand, the total number of snuff boxes I have in both hands is six. Or to translate the same truth into the characteristically modish and inelegant language of "numbers"[2] favoured by the more churlish mathematicians:

$$2+2 = 6$$

Point proven. Yet our present system of 'egalitarian' government, by which is really meant totalitarian rule by the proletarian hordes (many if not most of whom have dandruff) has convinced generations of citizens (their shoes in grave need of a polish) that the equation $2 + 2 = 4$ can somehow be made to hold water. Down this path lies madness. Next, they will be telling us that one and one makes two!!!

This grave mathematical deception, from which floweth the depraved and decadent condition of England today, must needs rightly be placed at the feet of Harold Wilson, who, far from

----

2 I am indebted to Professor Albert Einstein, a distant cousin of my stepmother's father-in-law, the 3rd Earl of Bessborough, for this information, for which I am happy to credit his tremendously brainy if overlong work "The Meaning of Relativity". Though Einstein persists in maintaining, for the most part, that two and two do indeed make four, I took from my reading of his book an entirely different lesson.

being an aristocrat, was the product of inferior breeding, misusing the adverb "hopefully" and never learning to hold his pipe in a manner befitting a gentleman.[3]

And, forsooth, how much has changed! When I first joined The Times as an apprentice leader-writer in 1950, all journalists on that newspaper were expected, quite rightly, to don top hat and tails at all times. Nor were we permitted to write our own articles, for it was considered an activity unfit for a gentleman. Instead, the necessary pieces were written for us by uniformed parlour maids, whom we would tip generously (sixpence ha'penny every Christmas) for their troubles. Never let it be said that there was a jot or tittle of snobbery about this. Like slavery, it was valued equally on both sides, allowing them to look up to us and, at one and the same time, us to look down on them.

Nowadays, to my certain knowledge, The Times is staffed almost exclusively by common people, many bussed in from the East End in boilersuits. Even Lord Rees-Mogg is obliged to adopt a flat cap, grubby overalls and a cockney accent before reporting for work. And a certain coarseness has crept into the prose. For instance, leading articles on the situation in Iraq invariably begin with the lamentable phraseology, "Fuck this for a game of soldiers". It all goes to show that equality may be a good thing in theory, but, like mathematics, it never works in practice.

Why are we so embarrassed by the notion of an aristocracy? Many of the most notable thinkers and philanthropists down the ages have been drawn from the aristocracy. Did not Lord Jesus

---

3 Wilson was once in attendance at a luncheon reception at which I was a guest; I noticed with horror that, imbibing his soup, he scooped his spoon towards him rather than away. The very next day, I saw it as no less than my duty to pen a passionate editorial column in which, having revealed this revolting social solecism, I called for his immediate resignation. This call, widely criticised at the time, nevertheless proved effective. Eighteen months later, Wilson resigned.

Christ hold a title?[4] And so too, in more recent times, do the Dukes of Hazzard. But since the war, successive shabby governments, preaching a meritocracy borne of envy and rancour, have seen to it that the aristocracy must huddle together in darkened rooms. Standards everywhere have thus slipped. Footballers no longer pass the ball in a gentlemanly fashion to their opponents, but seek instead to kick it into the goalmouth with brute force. Only yesterday, I heard of a youth who was not sporting a necktie on the "tube" train, yet will not face prosecution. Worse still, on the afternoon of September 11th 2001, I remember watching the television in mounting horror at the sight of the Mayor of New York appearing in public in a baseball cap.

Paradoxically, black is in fact white, and it follows on from there that white is black. It's as plain as the nose on the back of my hand. Yet egalitarian hypocrisy ensures that our children are taught the opposite, that in some strange way white is white, and black is black, and that you can't make an omelette without breaking eggs. If truth be told, my cousin the 4th Earl of Hartlepool assures me that he regularly makes an omelette without breaking eggs; he also takes care to employ too many cooks in order to improve his broth. In better days, he would have been appointed First Lord of the Treasury, and a very good thing too. As it is, he is bound into a straitjacket in a cripplingly expensive private rest home, yet another victim of this government's war against its social and intellectual superiors.

---

4 I believe his mother, Lady Mary, was one of the Virgins of Derbyshire, her family having been drawn to the Middle East by the clement climate some years previously.

Tony Benn

Sunday: Quite terrifying, really. I am woken by my wireless alarm clock, only to discover from the so-called newscaster that while I was asleep the Government has altered the time by an hour or more. Now they expect us to believe that 8 is really 7, that 6 is really 5, and so on.

It makes me absolutely sick. What an untrustworthy man Blair really is. Of course, the Establishment have always wanted it darker in the night, just so's ordinary decent working people will lose their bearings and trip up on kerbs, or walk slap into walls.

I expect the candle manufacturers put them up to it. And the more candles we have, the more likelihood there is of fire, causing a great many homes to burn down. Don't try and tell me the big guns of the construction industry haven't put Blair up to it.

Monday: I order a cab. "Hello," I say as I get in, "I'm Tony Benn." He looks me in the face, and the penny drops. "Golly gosh," he says, "You're Mr Tony Benn. Blow me down!" Without any sort of prompting, he has recognised me. I am tickled pink.

We engage in a tremendously stimulating discussion.

He tells me that the junction of Kensington High Street and Kensington Church Street has been blocked for three weeks now, due to roadworks. "I don't know what this country's coming to," he concludes.

I explain that the Establishment doesn't want the traffic to go any faster, because that would totally undermine the Government's secret time-changes yesterday, which were designed to remove an hour from ordinary people's lives. "You can tell M15 are behind most of these so called 'road-works'," I explain. "You can recognise them by their shiny yellow jackets and hard helmets."

"You should be Prime Minister," he says, as I pay the fare. What a fascinating discussion we have had, offering me much food for thought.

I take out a Polo Mint and put it in my ear. But I can't get a signal. Frankly, I'm beginning to suspect it is being deliberately jammed.

Tuesday: Now I hear that the brave Firefighters, lovely, decent lads, are going on strike to try and stop this whole ghastly business of the government's secret time-changes.

I pop into the local home furnishings store, march up to the bedding counter and ask for some Polos. They say they sell pillows, not Polos, and they show me one. "Well, I'll never be able to fit something that size in my ear!" I exclaim. What a bunch of proper charlies!

Eventually, I locate some Polo Mints at the sweet shop next door. "Do they come with batteries?" I ask, but it turns out these are extra, like so many things these days. So blow me down if they haven't even privatised Polo Mints! I have no wish to bring personalities into it, that's not my style, never has been, never will be, but I place the blame fairly and squarely on that smarmy, self-satisfied, grinning lickspittle Tony Blair.

The Education Secretary, Estelle Morris, on the television set at lunchtime. A bit effeminate, but forceful. It's quite obvious the Establishment is grooming him to take over from Blair in the next year or two. He'll be made Home Secretary next, then Chancellor. Talk of an impending resignation is pure misinformation.

Wednesday: Lovely note this morning from the Prime Minister, Tony Blair. What a super guy. He congratulated me on all my years in Parliament, and wished me well. He really is first-class, whatever the others might say, the greatest Labour leader since Attlee, whom I frankly never liked. "We may have had our differences in the past," I reply. "But I still have a great affection for you. Yours ever, Tony."

To distract attention from the mess they're making in Iraq, the Bush administration has sent its own hit-man to Washington, and he's now picking ordinary citizens off on direct orders from the White House. And of course all this Ulrika Jonsson to-do is part-and-parcel of the same thing. Don't tell me she's not an undercover MI5 operative: former TV-am weathercasters always are, in my experience.

Thursday: Tea with Martin McGuinness. Lovely man. Really super warm smile. Wouldn't hurt a fly. "I frankly deplore the way this Government allows its media to describe you as a terrorist, Martin," I say, pouring him another cuppa. I can't help but notice he's fiddling with something. "What's that you've got there, Martin?" I ask, with a chuckle.

"It's a fly, Tony," he replies with that lovely Irish lilt of his. "I'm

179

just pulling its wings off. For its own good, of course."

"Quite!" I say. "It's probably sick to death of all that flying nonsense. They work them far too hard. Needs a well-earned rest, eh?"

Having finished pulling the wings off, Martin kindly squashes the fly flat as a pancake, "to put it out of its misery". What a really super, kindly chap he is. A tear comes into my eye when I think of this great act of kindness he has performed on a little fly.

"No life for a fly, without wings," I say, reassuringly, and we hug one another.

Early Christmas card from Augusto Pinochet, "to the best Leader the Labour Party never had!" I'm tickled pink, obviously. Very sweet of him. What a nice old man he really is. In the past, we had our differences, but I now feel a very real affection for the guy. So much more genuine than that dreadful little phony Tony Blair, for instance.

Friday: Now that I've left the Commons, I can begin to engage in real politics! This morning, I was out in the garden with m'bricks and m'cement, attempting to rebuild the Berlin Wall, which is still greatly missed. The Cold War was, let's face it, a war against socialism – and it's not a war I intend to lose. Early days yet, of course, but I plan to take the wall from Holland Park, through Oxford Circus, across the Channel to Hamburg, on to Berlin, then all the way through to China. I'll have to keep an eye open for Jonsson and her sniper friends, of course – but with Inspector Morse on our side and a fresh packet of Polo Mints in our pocket, believe me, there'll be no stopping us.

Anne Robinson

Sit up straight, class, and answer me this one: which sassy lady has the highest-rated TV quiz show among the all-important 19-49 age group in the US of A?

Right first time: moi.

I am, to coin a phrase, the strongest link. Okay, if you really want to know what I earned last year I will tell you – with some reluctance! It was a seven figure sum – and a lot closer, I might add, to $3m than to $2m. Alright, it was $2,765,402 to be exact, and if you don't believe me, go ask my top international Manhattan-based accountant.

Yes, I own a stately pile in Gloucestershire, with its own 40-foot kitchen and top-of-the-range designer cooker, a Henry Moore in the solarium, a Lucian Freud in the luxury fitted bathroom (with bidet and whirlpool bath) and an indoor swimming pool with full sauna facilities to match. I count top stars like Roger Moore,

Michael Winner, Roseanne Barr and top chef Keith Floyd among my closest friends – and I don't blink an eyelid when I walk into Bergdorf Goodman in Manhattan and emerge twenty minutes later, $15,000 the poorer.

For all her screaming and shouting and getting her proverbial knickers in a twist, that's something Germaine Greer can't claim. Incidentally, Germaine, a visit to a top hair salon might not go amiss – remind me to give you the number of mine, he's a sweety (though – sorry, love – I suspect he'd run a mile from you and your bird's nest!).

HISTORICAL FOOTNOTE: In the very same week I was approached by the BBC to host its flagship consumer programme Watchdog, Germaine signed on for her umpteenth year as some sort of lecturer at Warwick University at a salary of zilch. So much for the Feminist Movement!

So who am I? Who's the REAL Annie? That's the question on everyone's lips. The highest-paid woman journalist in Britain – or the biggest TV celebrity America's ever seen? Or, to put it another way – will the real Anne Robinson please stand up?!?!

These days, I'm probably best known for my wickedly funny repartee on the top-rated "Weakest Link". It's an open secret that some of my barbed gems have already entered all the major quotation books:

"So, Gary, call yourself a plumber? You've really plumbed the depths this time, haven't you?!!!!!!"

"So, Susan, you're not very clever after all!!!!!"

"Have you ever heard the phrase, 'you're utterly useless', then, Simon?"

What's the Queen on, these days? Not much more than £1 million, if the truth be told.

And that doesn't take you very far. Not these days it doesn't.

We may be rivals, but frankly I feel sorry for her.

I really do.

Frankly, I wouldn't do her job for all the dosh in the world. Not if they begged me I wouldn't.

So why's she not negotiated a better deal for herself, that's what I want to know?

Personally, I blame the parents. They brought her up in a lah-di-dah toffee-nosed silver-spoon world where it was considered vulgar, don't you know, to talk cash.

So now when she's in the perfect bargaining position, and by my reckoning she could quadruple her annual income overnight, what does the good lady do? Precisely nothing.

She just sits on her backside. And waves.

I am frankly growing thoroughly sick and frankly tired of single-handedly life-coaching generations of females. Pleading with them not to be so weedy about demanding the rise they deserve.

Let's face it. The Queen is in a superb position to develop an enhanced worldwide marketing strategy. The lady's got it all. Widespread international media profile. Face on all the stamps. Close friend of the rich and famous. Millionaire lifestyle. The lot.

And she possesses the one advertising tool money can't buy. Trust. And dignity. Which makes two.

I hate to see the woman earning so much less than me. So I offer her this four-point plan for free:

1) TV deal (eg hosting upmarket lifestyle show) – £7m.

2) Worldwide advertising deal (eg Oil of Olay) – £4.5m.

3) Signature HMQ comprehensive lingerie and eveningwear range – £6.3m.

4) Combined Kiss-and-Tell memoirs, full serialisation rights plus no-holds-barred 6-part TV interview series with Oprah – £8.4m. Go for it, Lilibet. And soon you'll be eating at the top table with the rest of us.

Anyone else noticed how our policemen are getting younger?

So. Adam Faith. Has died. And he was only just past 60.

Sad – but so much for the staying power of the male of the species!

Get up and go? In Adam's case, it's got up and gone, more like.

I met the bloke once. And very fanciable he was too, for a titch. I was enjoying lunch in a highly expensive restaurant with two multi-millionaires at the time. Thoroughly amusing them with tales of my classic meeting with the Princess Royal, Cilla (don't knock her – Penrose guesstimates she must be worth upwards of £63 million) and the splendid Barry Perkins of Casualty fame.

Adam was at the next table. From the look of him, he couldn't wait to talk to yours truly. So I eventually went up to his table. And introduced myself.

He looked suitably chuffed. "Are you after an autograph?" he said. So I got out my pen and gave him one.

But now he's the Weakest Link. Goodbye!